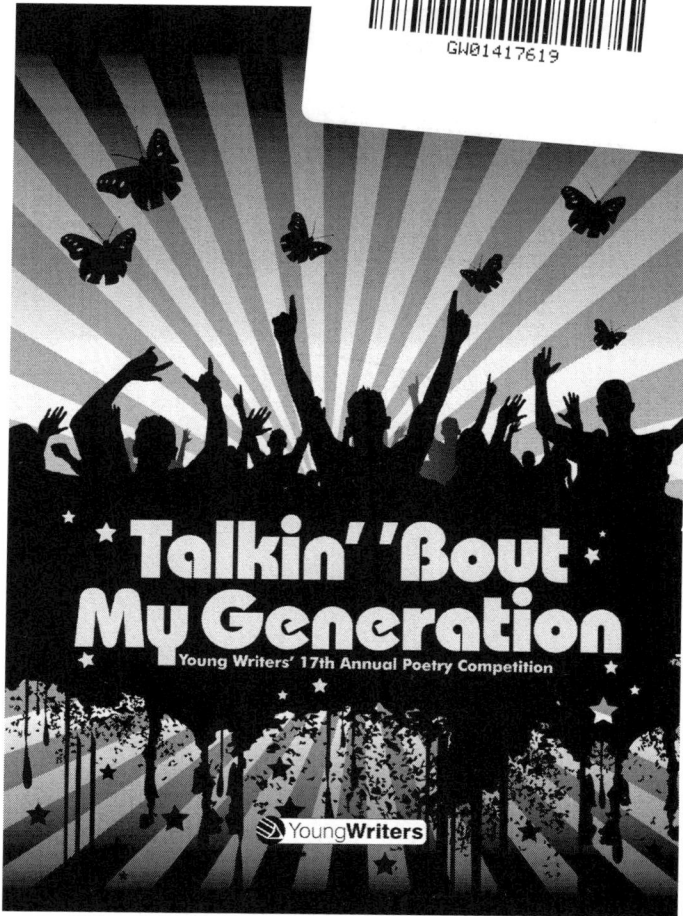

Talkin' 'Bout My Generation

Young Writers' 17th Annual Poetry Competition

YoungWriters

Cumbria

Edited by Annabel Cook

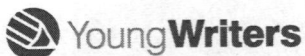

Young**Writers**

First published in Great Britain in 2008 by:
Young Writers
Remus House
Coltsfoot Drive
Peterborough
PE2 9JX
Telephone: 01733 890066
Website: www.youngwriters.co.uk

SB ISBN 978-1 84431 427 0

Foreword

This year, the Young Writers' *Talkin' 'Bout My Generation* competition proudly presents a showcase of the best poetic talent selected from thousands of up-and-coming writers nationwide.

Young Writers was established in 1991 to promote the reading and writing of poetry within schools and to the young of today. Our books nurture and inspire confidence in the ability of young writers and provide a snapshot of poems written in schools and at home by budding poets of the future.

The thought, effort, imagination and hard work put into each poem impressed us all and the task of selecting poems was a difficult but nevertheless enjoyable experience.

We hope you are as pleased as we are with the final selection and that you and your family continue to be entertained with *Talkin' 'Bout My Generation Cumbria* for many years to come.

Contents

Rebecca Allen (12)	38
Hazel Furniss (13)	39
Vicki Richards (11)	40
Tonicha Grady (11)	41
Conor Mulholland (11)	42
Olivia Thoburn (11)	43
Hannah Stobart (11)	44
Ananta Handley (11)	45
Adam Davidson (11)	46
Abigail Strong (11)	47
Chris Gracey (12)	48
Helen Brown (12)	49
Jon Smith (12)	50
Ryan Bird (12)	51
James Metcalfe (13)	52
Sam Richards (14)	53
Luke Andrews (11)	54
Emily Clarke (12)	55
Victoria Neil (15)	56
Charlotte James (14)	57
Harriet Coulthard (14)	58
Laura Webster (14)	59
Corinne Irving (14)	60
Eleanor Preston (14)	61
Becca Lamb (16)	62
Martin Hall (12)	63
Timothy Cottingham (17)	64
Amy Dawes (13)	65
Allicia Corry (12)	66
Angharad Percival (12)	67
Ben Hodgson (12)	68
Jamie Foster (12)	69
Ashleigh Hunter (12)	70
Matthew Boak (12)	71
Helen Little (12)	72
Danielle Sharpe (12)	73
Matthew Coates (12)	74
John McBride (17)	75
Alice Simpson (13)	76
James Taylor (14)	77
Tim Perry (13)	798
Philip Watts (13)	80

Jeni Rogers (14)	81
Alex Magill (13)	82
Kelly-Louise Harding (13)	83
Christian Drake (13)	84
Emma Armstrong (13)	85
Rebecca Graham (13)	86
Tavia Davies (13)	87
Emma Dickinson (13)	88
Claire Allison (13)	89
Amy Dugdale (14)	90
Jordyn Johnston (13)	91
Andy Butcher (14)	92
Jack Shannon (13)	93
Laura Potts (13)	94
Jaki Watt (14)	95
Shelley Teasdale (13)	96
Bethan Daltrey (16)	97
Lauren Coulthard (12)	98
Georgina Goddard (16)	99
Sarah Penrice (17)	100
Katie Walker & Francesca Patterson (16)	101
Jodie Foster (16)	102
Peter Allison (12)	103
Shannon Bell (12)	104

St Joseph's Catholic High School,
Business & Enterprise College, Workington

Lauren Foskett (11)	105
Mathew Poole (11)	106
Hannah Scott (11)	107
Kirsty Wright (15)	108
Abbie Martin (15)	109
Sarah Williamson (13)	110
Jessica Lee (12)	111
Karl Monkhouse (13)	112
Jordan Cameron (13)	113
Becky McQuire (14)	114
Shannon Jennings (12)	115
Daniel Grierson (12)	116
Megan Davy (12)	117
Lewis Pettit (13)	118

Tom Fisher (13) 161
Rebecca Burgess (13) 162
Ryan Lea (12) 163
Melissa Armstrong (12) 164
Melanie West (12) 165
Carl Robertson (12) 166
Rebecca Hunt (12) 167
Melissa Bathgate (12) 168
Claire Linford (13) 169
Chelsea Ritson (12) 170
Nathan Graham (12) 171
Oliver Penn (11) 172
Shannon Stuart (11) 173
Luke Norman (11) 174
Jessica Ellis (11) 175
Calvin Hodgson (12) 176
Courtney Cannell (11) 177
Naomi Peet (12) 178
Rebecca Dolan (12) 179
Maria Varghese (12) 180
Aiméé Stewart (12) 181
Andrew Shillito (12) 182
Bethany Lines (12) 183
Vivien Ng (12) 184
Edi Akpan (11) 185
Liam Cooper (11) 186
James Taylor (11) 187
Bethany Burdon (11) 188
Emma Suitor (11) 189
Georgia Dickinson (11) 190
Joshua Jardine (11) 191
Hannah Aitken (12) 192

Ullswater Community College

Hagen Moss (12) 193
Kieran Birkett (11) 194
Holly Streatfield (11) 195
Connie Dalton (11) 196
Anya Wilcock (11) 197
Adam Weir (11) 198
Ross Kirkbride (11) 199

The Poems

Talkin' 'Bout My Generation

This is our generation:

There are girls who wear a little too much blush and foundation.
Boys who get high off a sugar rush and lose realisation.
Chavs that drink cider they found on the train.
Teenagers who nearly always complain,
Emos that look like they've cut their hair with a lawnmower.
Geeks whose eyes whirl and blare when the teacher sets them
                                        extra maths homework.
Rebels who hurl chips at old people.
Lads who don't do as they're told and just say you wouldn't
                                understand you're too old!

This is our generation I'm sorry to say if you don't like it go away!

Struan Robinson (13)
Austin Friars St Monica's School

Talkin' 'Bout My Generation

Yeah you might think we're thugs,
Drinkin' beer,
And takin' drugs,
Fillin' all you lot with fear.

But under all this clothing,
The clothing that we wear,
That makes you oh so loathing,
Even including our hair.

Under this skin and bone,
We're not all cyber-freaks,
That always play on phones,
And that talk in teen speak.

So stop saying all the things about us,
Believing these lies in the news,
Stop making all this fuss,
'Cause you used to be on the booze.

Alex Taylor (13)
Austin Friars St Monica's School

My Generation!

We don't all use drugs
Look at your generation
And think again.

We don't all drink beer
In fact, adults drink more
Still criticising?

We don't all text loads
Our heads attached to our phones
Adults text as much.

We don't always eat
Filling our stomachs with crisps
Some can't and won't eat.

We don't all sleep in
Till late in the afternoon
From drinking last night.

We're not all racist
Prejudice against people
We accept others.

We don't constantly
Watch our TVs with square eyes
We can walk and run.

We are not all thieves
We're not all violent hoodies
Smashing in windows.

We do care a lot
This is our generation
Accept how we are.

Harriet Potts (12)
Austin Friars St Monica's School

My Generation!

Yo yo yo!
This is my generation!
Emos, nerds, chavs
I got a new PlayStation!

Wuzzup bro?
Live life to the max!
TopShop, New Look
Who cares about tax?

Come on guys!
Let's get some awesome mates!
Test 'til dawn, lie-in
Get to school late!

What ya bin up ta?
I'm getting an mp3!
It beats your crappy iPod!
It's just me, me, me!

So that's it! Gottit?
The DVD, the CD rom
We'll rock your socks!
This age is the bomb!

Amy Hill (13)
Austin Friars St Monica's School

Talkin' 'Bout My Generation

I am a cool hoodie,
My generation rocks,
I like to wear my trousers,
Tucked into my socks,

I am a teenager,
I like to grunt and groan,
If someone asks me something,
I'll answer with a moan,

What's up yo minted cool dude,
You really need to chill,
If you need some help to do it,
Then simply take a pill,

Check out the new Xbox,
The graphics make me drool,
The Game Cube and the PlayStation.
Are awesomely like cool,

I see you 'cross the street,
But I'll ring you anyway,
Want to watch the telly,
Since it's such a lovely day,

Look at my new iPod,
The colour is the best,
If you think yours is better,
Then come on give me a rest!

William Low (12)
Austin Friars St Monica's School

My Generation!

Now, the youth of today
We really couldn't care.
About school, nor homework
Or anyone, anywhere!

We're hip, we're hard
We reckon that we are 'it'.
We're ignorant and smelly
We could not care a bit!

We're spotty, we're stupid
We're grossly overweight.
We're always glued to TVs
Or texting our best mate!

We dress like scruffy chavs
We think we're 18.
We're chatting up the lasses
Or slapping on the spot cream!

Alcohol and cigarettes
We think this is propa cool.
Grebs on their skateboards
Look like utter fools!

Nerds with their bow ties
Emos with lots of scars.
Chavs with their Burberry
And the freaks that see stars!

Now our generation
It's actually pretty fun,
But just guess where we got it from
And that's my poem done!

Josh Barton (12)
Austin Friars St Monica's School

Talkin' 'Bout My Generation

My generation love the PlayStation
We have games an' stuff
There are clothes and homes.
With mobile phones.
Chavs and freaks
As well as geeks

We have TVs with Sky,
Food and pie.
Days at school where we rule.
Sports and thoughts.
Words and chords

Wanna hear some talk
That wat u want?
U l8ter
We txt all day an
Talk away.

U wanna 'ear more
We walk da walk
An' talk da talk
We know the fashion
And it's a passion.

Where u goin'
Ne getting borin'?
Wuzzup wid ya?
Ya not noin
Eh were ya goin'?

Surf the net
Wiz the kid
Find it out
Watch out
My generation are knowing.

Rachel Brass (12)
Austin Friars St Monica's School

Our Generation

Yo! Wot up?
U got dat new song, bro?
Nah dude, not yet . . . text u wen I do tho . . .
Deffo!

Txtin and Linin
Drinking 'nd dealing
Chattin' and surfin'
All this stuff is our generation!

Ohmigod! the Big Brother final was
Quality last nite . . .
Yer I no . . . rite? It was dead good . . .
Tripple cringe!

New words in . . .
Old ones out . . .
Technology . . . wham!
iPods, PlayStations, MSN mobiles . . .
All this stuff is our generation!

Shoppin' sprees rock . . .
Don't wanna hear 'I'm tired'
Deal with it!
All these shops are in it . . .
Let's 'ave our generation!

Vanessa Brown (12)
Austin Friars St Monica's School

Our Generation

Chavs, emos, swats and goths,
Our generation has them all.
Choirboys and tough rock bands,
Music loud and shrilly.
Slamming door and being rude
And robbing grandmas' handbags.
No one ever really knows
Just how far we'll go,
Some are good
Some are bad
Mixed in all together.
Texts and phones
Have split us up
And PSPs aren't helping
Many people moan we're fat,
But waddle on right past us.
People shout and run around
Guess who we take after?
Parents prowl and moan complaints
But we don't give a laughter.
Dogs and cats we want them both,
But hate them two days after.
But all deep down
You cannot frown
Because it's you that we take after.

Patrick Everingham (12)
Austin Friars St Monica's School

Our Generation

Our generation, we're always getting told,
No one's better than the old,
Always saying we have no respect,
And that we are a great big threat.
We always play music way too loud,
Our parents telling us it's not allowed,
We strut around saying 'we're better',
'Don't mess with us or we'll get yer,'
We all get thrown out of shops and places,
All saying that we're huge disgraces.

Our generation, we have all the gadgets,
Mobiles, laptops and robotic pets,
We spend our free time on MSN,
Chatting to our mates again and again.
We always want the newest stuff,
But our parents say it's a load of guff,
We all complain that we're hard done to,
Our parents say they were, not you.
Nobody trusts us they keep well away,
But we don't care we just stay.

Our generation, we have gangs and cliques,
There are the rebels and computer geeks,
The emos and the ASBOs,
They have no friends just foes,
The vandals and the swats,
All trying to be what they're not,
Bragging about all the scars they've got,
But who cares what,
We're the best you're not,
Our generation.

Edward Ball (13)
Austin Friars St Monica's School

Talkin' 'Bout My Generation

Talkin' 'bout my generation,
Nobody gets it right,
All they see is da drugs and booze,

No struggle in life,
We get what we want on
Silver platters,
We is da reigning family

Even da coppers are frightened to charge,
Cos we be fierce and cruel,
Breaking up their families,
Ruining their lives,

What 'bout da little grannies,
Bars on da windows,
Frightened to go out,
We don't care 'bout them,

Da streets are fighting
Not just us,
They live with the paint,
But not the blood,

No one knows how to break out,
Of this life
We is trapped,
By snares
Hungry for our blood,
The riots,
The street fights,
The anger,
The hate,
The despair.

Catriona Duff (13)
Austin Friars St Monica's School

My Generation

Our generation are always being told,
Do what you're told.
We try to gain the most respect,
The ones our parents don't detect.
We always try to find a date,
But then we find out it's too late.
We always pretend that we bought,
Until we're found out or caught.
We cause havoc around the place,
Until the police solve the case.
We play the music people hate,
They put a smile on our dull face.
We always try to look real hard,
Until our parents play the card
This is our generation!

We always like to eat fast food,
Then we finish with some booze.
We smoke and take some drugs,
People sometimes say we're mugs.
We have our mobiles which look real cool,
Not many people call us fools.
We have our style and all that,
With our cool Burberry caps.
Our consoles are the best,
They keep us away from our beds.
We hang around the nightclubs,
And sometimes in the pub.
Me and my gang are the best,
We control all the west,
This is our generation!

Stephen Hagan (12)
Austin Friars St Monica's School

My Generation

There are many factions in modern day youth, which all have their own names. Here is a useful rhyme in which to remember them.

We are happily busy humming,
At the scally who is coming,
And pretty soon we will be running,
From the chav beside me lulling,
And the emos are a mulling,
For their blood they are now culling.
From their arms which they are cutting,
At the glam queens who are strutting,
Around the shops which are busy shutting
And the nerds they are a putting,
Their books which now are jutting,
Over gangsters who are gutting,
The poor golfer who was putting,
Now is in hospital.

Peter Relph (15)
Austin Friars St Monica's School

Talkin' 'Bout My Generation

Generation after generation,
Our generation is a celebration,
Celebrating the make of the TV,
Soon there'll be robots making cups of tea.

Our generation's the best,
Sending quick emails and texts,
Language is changing,
Cuz of TXT msgN.

Our generation has the best technology,
Cars and phones, we don't need mythology
Our generation is the best,
We are all better than the rest.

Pui Yu Liu (12)
Austin Friars St Monica's School

My Generation

(This poem was written to prove that not all people of our generation are fools like the person I pretend to be in this poem!)

Wassup!
How's it down in the ghetto?
Rockin' out down at Netto!
You know you want to be like us!
So come on down and start to cuss.

We all live down on the estate,
And no longer know how to conjugate,
With our iPods and Xboxes and a PS3
We no longer need Panorama on the BBC.

We are all solid, we are rock hard,
Nuff said, we ain't getting scarred,
So when you see us beating old grannies,
We will get in her purse's nooks and crannies,

Don't mess with us, don't mess our formation,
Cos our words are so cool, you'll need a translation,
We'll rule the world; we'll be so cool,
So don't mess with us, you thick-headed fool!

Ben Hodgkiss (14)
Austin Friars St Monica's School

We're Not Really That Bad!

Our generation has a really bad name
Like we think our life is just a killing game
But we're not really like that; it's the honest truth
Just look at my friends if you want the proof

People think that all we do is hang out in big gangs
That we're all really evil, like we've just grown fangs
But in truth it's not like that, we just like shopping in town
And we really don't like it when we get old fogey's frowns

So now do you believe me that we're really not that bad?
Even though we may annoy you as well as Mum and Dad
And next time you see us out and about
Bear it in mind that we don't want a fight.

Sarah Calvert (13)
Austin Friars St Monica's School

My Generation

Yo! What's hanging?
The teen's generation?
Oh, it's iPods and mobiles
It's all the new creation!
Dossin' in town,
Hanging with 'the crew',
Online messaging
Finding out what's new!
Orite! What's up?
The teen's generation?
Oh, it's raving and rocking,
It's all the new creation!
Stuffing the homework,
Shoving the books,
There's wack days,
Are all about the looks!
Hey what's the crack?
The new generation?
Oh, it's late nights and lie-ins,
It's all the new creation!
Whistling at girls,
Chatting up boys,
Banging late parties,
Growing out of toys!
The teen's generation
It's the latest goss,
Don't go dissin' us,
Hey! It's your loss!

Ellie Margerison (12)
Austin Friars St Monica's School

Talkin' 'Bout My Generation

Chain smoking, foul-mouthed, ASBOs,
Yes, it is the chavs, the school bullies everyone fears,
All competing to be the 'hardest',
Teacher's worst enemy as they come with an attitude,
With a capital A.

Innocent, giggly, backstabbers,
OMG, it's the girly girls, cheering the latest chants,
Passion for fashion,
Loves everyone to their totally pretty little faces,
Hating behind backs.

Long haired, chilled and random,
Of course, it's the grebs talking a load of rubbish,
Not bothered about popularity,
Loving rock music longing to see their favourite group,
Rock on.

Desperate, loathing and popularity craving,
Obviously, it's the wannabes, tiptoeing up the popularity ladder,
No threat to anyone,
Constantly untrue to themselves, trying to be something they're not,
Living a lie.

Fit, rough and sport orientated,
Ohh, it's the footie boys, showing off their jaw-dropping skills,
Only ever interested in their football,
'Match of the Day' eat your heart, the footie boys know best,
Dedication for life.

Plain Janes, normal and mysterious,
Don't forget the ungrouped people, can be shy but there is no
stereotype,
Not worried about where they are popularity wise,
Good all-rounders but you never know what happens after school,
A little secretive.

Teacher's pet, model students and guarded,
Miss, Miss, it's the swots, calculators at hand,
Obsessed with future career,
Mummy's boys, Daddy's girls their biggest social life is family,
Yawn.

Emily Mechie (14)
Caldew School

Talkin' 'Bout Our Generation

Talking about our generation,
Can cause a lot of complication.
All the technology is really cool,
Apart from when you're not allowed to use it in school.
Nintendo Wii, iPods and the PlayStation,
Have all really filled our nation.
The people have also changed from all being the same.
Girlie girls, grebos, goths and jocks but that is just a name.
Chavs, emos, geeks and swots,
Were all the same when they were just tots.
DVD and film are a whole different story,
Romcom, thriller, comedy, horror and gory.
They are all really good in their own different ways,
Just like the generations which will never fail to amaze.

Ellen Rogerson (14)
Caldew School

Generation

Hanging around with black hoodies and trackies
My friends on their bikes giving me backies,
Hopping, skipping, jumping and running
Quick, all hide the old witch is coming,
Getting up to mischief and giving our parents a whole load of grief,
Listening to MC and acting all sweet,
From moving and grooving and jumping all about,
In your room to sitting on your balcony and watching the moon

Hanging around with a little spray can
Covering the walls with a whole load of slang,
Meeting your friends at the park late at night
Waiting for people to give them a fright,
Hopping, skipping, running and jumping ready to give someone
a great big thumping,
Sitting at home watching the telly with a big pile of chocolate feeding
my belly.

(Yummy) (Yummy).

Demi Queen (11)
Caldew School

Now I Am Old My Things Are Great!

I like my train,
I like my deep hot bath with a duck and boat,
I like my washer going round and round,
I like my pram,
I like my car mat.
But
Now I am old,
I like my iPod,
I like my telly,
I like my phone,
I like my computer,
And I like my friends.
I might be old but still feel as young as a bird.

Ben Montgomery (11)
Caldew School

50 Years Ago

50 years ago, you used to go out and play
Now you sit in your chair all day
50 years ago, you used to have long blonde hair
Now you don't even care
50 years ago, you used to be kind
Now your friends have left you behind
50 years ago, you were never at home
Now you are all alone.

Matthew Robinson (14)
Caldew School

My Generation

Some models are skinny
We like how they look,
We want what they have
So we change.

Some actors are violent
We copy their style,
We do what they do
So adults lose trust.

Because of the way we act
They jump to conclusions,
They don't understand
How that makes us feel,
Because we're misunderstood,
My generation.

Lauren Bowman (14)
Caldew School

My Generation Different

In my generation, we address the nation how we want.
We hang about and play on games that your generation could
only dream about.
We don't repress or stress and we always leave a mess.
When we graffiti we don't worry about repairs.
We pay attention less in classes in school.
And we definitely see a lot more separations.
We get a lot more detentions.
And we've got no apprehensions.

In your generation you addressed the nation with utmost politeness.
Your games used to be skipping and jacks.
You would never repress and you were always stressed
and you never left a mess.
Your graffiti was chalk on the floor and you were more bothered
about declarations.
To pay more attention in school and to get the cane.
And you never, never asked for more.
You were full of apprehensions.

But maybe we aren't that different.
I have MSN and you had your pen to write to your pal you met
down in London.
I have a dog and you had a frog.
And we both certainly made dens.
And to our mothers we were nothing but little gems.
I do my work on a computer you on a stool with paper
and a fountain pen.
We both think we'll never get old.
But you did and I will and you've earned your fair share of gold
So maybe we aren't that different maybe we are the same.
Only maybe the same developed over 50 years and everything
just seems different.

Matthew Hodgson (14)
Caldew School

The Way We Are

We walk down the street with music in our ears.
Which by the way I have pierced.
Mobiles out texting away,
Talking to friends all through the day.
Shopping with mates bought a new hoodie,
I've got footy tomorrow hope I don't get muddy.
Turn the radio up, my favourite song's on.
Song's finished and I'm gone.
Party tonight, new outfit,
I can't wait it's going to be mint.
Party's over it was great fun,
School tomorrow and I'll probably get done.

Jessica Carruthers (15)
Caldew School

Anthem

(Snapshots of lyrics from songs by Goo Goo Dolls)

Now this angry little girl
Drowning in this petty world
Swallow all your bitter pills
That's what makes you beautiful
I don't need what you ain't got
Now I can't believe it's coming true
God it's good to be alive
And I'm still waiting here for you
I'm aware
I'm in love but you don't care.

Killing myself from the inside out
I wished for things that I don't need
All I wanted
I get scared but I'm not crawling on my knees
It's easy to forget, yeah
When you choke on a regret, yeah
Who the hell did I think I was?
I'm not sure where I belong
Nowhere's home and I'm all alone
And I wasn't all the things I tried to make believe I was
All the empty things disguised as me.

You're the closest to heaven that I'll ever be
And I don't wanna go home right now
Sooner or later it's over
I just don't wanna miss you tonight.

Coz tonight's the night the world begins again.

Cheryl Fleming (16)
Caldew School

I'll Do It My Way

Ain't no reason things are this way,
It's how they've always been and how they intend to stay
I can't explain why we live this way,
We do it every day
Preachers on the podiums speaking of saints,
Prophets on the sidewalks begging for change,
And you from the rooftops, cursing my name.

Who are you to judge me?
Telling me my rights,
When they're your rights too!

Prison walls still standing tall,
Some things never change at all.
Keep building prisons, going to fill them all,
Working your fingers bare to the bone;
Breaking your back, making you sell your soul.
I know what stories you've told,
So there's no reason to be so cold!

Ain't no reason things are this way.
It's how they've always been and how they intend to stay.
You keep whining and I'll live my day,
I just can't explain why we live this way
But I'll do it anyway.

Anna McCrone (16)
Caldew School

Talkin' 'Bout My Generation!

All about teens of today . . .

Play

T roublesome teens
E nergetic
E ntertain themselves
N icotine addictions

Pause
Wait there's more . . .
Play

A dults to come
G ormless
E gos too big to handle
R eputations
S ex, drugs and rock 'n' roll.

Stop.

Sarah Jackson (15)
Caldew School

Talking About My Generation

Rap, hip hop, indie, trance,
Metal, rock, R&B, dance,
Jazz, grunge, blues, MC,
Folk, techno, classical, country.

Chav, goth, greb, preppy,
Wannabe, emo, alternative, geeky,
Skater, scene, nerd, scally,
Punk, indie, rocker, normally?

Action, romantic, comedy, crime,
Drama, adventure, horror, sci-fi,
War, western, gangster, fantasy,
Animated, family, musical, mystery.

Red, green, pink, yellow,
Maroon, rose, scarlet, indigo,
Orange, purple, blue, beige,
Black, magenta, lilac, jade.

England, France, Wales, Scotland,
America, Australia, Greece, Ireland,
Japan, Brazil, Turkey, Jamaica,
Spain, Cuba, Cyprus, Argentina.

You can be anyone, anywhere, anytime, anyhow,
Because this modern generation,
Is all about now.

Emma Whitfield (14)
Caldew School

My Generation . . .

In my generation things have moved on,
In much more many ways than one,
We now have things like MSN,
To talk to our friends and instead of using a pen.

iPods, laptops and the latest phone,
Without these we are unknown,
We all need our plasma TVs,
No one can live without one of these.

Everybody wants to be like the celebrities,
Seen in all the magazines,
Covered from top to toe,
From the latest fashion show.

Trips to the cinema every weekend,
Money from parents we have to lend,
Going to town on a shopping spree,
Nothing sounds better to me.

In my generation things have moved on,
In much more many ways than one.

Amy Dickinson (14)
Caldew School

60 Years Ago . . .

60 years ago there were big phones,
60 years ago there was no telly,
60 years ago we went to play,
60 years ago we wore blazers to school,
60 years ago is nothing like now.

In 2007 there are small mobiles,
In 2007 you can wear whatever you want to school,
In 2007 there are millions of TVs,
In 2007 you play on your PlayStation,
2007 is nothing like back then.

Sam Smith (11)
Caldew School

My Generation

Mobile phones pretty and pink,
Yellow hairbands and a cute boy's wink.

Girly shops from the local streets,
Enjoyable gifts and tasty treats.
Noisy little sisters are so not cool,
Elephant slipper and a big swimming pool.
Rosy apples from the corner shop,
Arcade music and a cute bunny's hop.
Tank tops and fizzy drinks,
Ink gel pens and Saturday nights watching the Weakest Links.
Ozzy Osbourne, my grandad's fav tune.
Naughty tricks from my older brother and my best friend
Acting like a loon.

Tamara Davenport (11)
Caldew School

My Generation

By the amount of our generation who go out shoe shopping
It won't only be the prices that are dropping.
Shoes, shoes, so many to choose, heels, slingbacks and pumps.
They lie in a mall, a shop or a stall some beautiful and some not.
Wedges, boots and stilettos too.
Unpopular ones lying alone by themselves at home.
I have always wondered why people have an urge to buy shoes
that do not fit them because they are nice, but by the time they do fit
they are out and something else is in so they get thrown in the bin.

Cara Cormack (11)
Caldew School

My Generation

Computers and phones and MSN
This is my generation.
Laptops and Wiis and DSs and trampolines
This is my generation
Swimming and dancing and other sport
This is my generation
CDs and medals and all in one swimming suits
This is my generation
So here I come.

Alix Lancaster (11)
Caldew School

My Generation

Plasma TVs
And PS3s,
iPods, along with mp3s,
That's my generation.
Mums and dads had cassettes,
Vinyl records, they were the best.
They had Commodore 64,
Now it's laptops and so much more.
Dial-up phones are a thing of the past,
Mobile phones are here to last.
Technology changes day by day,
But family and friends are here to stay.

Lucy Wilkinson (11)
Caldew School

My Generation

Why do all the older people hate us?
Do they think we're all the same?
What do they think we are?
And why are we always blamed?

Why do the younger people hate us?
Do they think we're all the same?
Do they hate our hair and clothes?
Or our Zimmer frames?

Kate Graham (12)
Caldew School

My Generation Is

My generation is:
Having the latest fashion,
The newest mobile,
Having sweets and fizzy drinks,
iPods, TVs, PlayStations,
Christmas present madness,
Going to the cinema, town and ice rinks!

My generation will be different to yours,
Mine has a lot of technology, noise and laws.
My mum, grandma, brother and dad,
Different generations future and past.
A new generation opens all the time.

What do you have in your generation that I don't have in mine?

Rebecca Allen (12)
Caldew School

What Am I?

iPods
CDs
Laptop
15 inch Plasma
Mobiles
McDonald's
Big Mac - no thanks
Burberry
Fred Perry
Helly Hanson
Yobs
Chavs
Skinny jeans (black)
Hoodies
Earrings
Studs
My generation is this all it can be,
Why am I judged, can't I just be me
By Hazel Furniss
Chav free zone!

Hazel Furniss (13)
Caldew School

When I Was Young

When I was young we didn't have
Computers, mobiles, grebos or chavs,
We used to run and laugh and play
Not sit around watching TV all day.

When I was young we didn't use
These computer systems to amuse
We'd jump around and laugh and sing
We never used to need no bling.

When I was young we didn't care
About having lovely and straight hair,
We used to sit and curl it all
Not stand and straighten it in the hall.

Everything has changed since I was young
That was my generation.

Vicki Richards (11)
Caldew School

My Nana

I have a TV
I have a PS2
I have a mobile, iPod and Game Boy

Talking about my generation

My nana doesn't have a TV
My nana doesn't have a PS2
My nana doesn't have a mobile, iPod or a Game Boy

My nana has a book

Talking about my generation.

Tonicha Grady (11)
Caldew School

My Generation

Being young is cool and fun
It makes us feel so small inside.
Being young is like a new life
Being young like a giant
Being young feels like an ant.

Old people just think we are mugs
It makes us feel like we have no buds,
They think we are chavs
They think we are yobos
But people my age, some of us are not.

Conor Mulholland (11)
Caldew School

My Generation

Mobile phones with minted tones,
Plasma TVs and mp3,
That's my generation.

We don't like to talk
We just like to text
I wonder what will come out next
That's my generation.

12 foot trampolines in everyone's garden,
But when we burp very few say pardon,
That's my generation.

We all want the latest stuff
But if we don't get it,
We go in a huff
That's my generation.

All the kids are great on the net,
And when parents come to do it they always forget,
That's my generation.

Olivia Thoburn (11)
Caldew School

My Generation

Buying many new things
Is one of my favourite things
Helping my mum and dad
Playing with my brother
No I don't do that
I have other things to do

Go outside sit with my friends
Chatting about things we do best
Adults go by
Keeping a close eye
What should we do next?

Things they do look so cold
I wish to die before I get old
Why don't you fade away?
Or hear us say
Grown ups they're so boring.

Hannah Stobart (11)
Caldew School

My Generation

M y generation
Y et to go

G oing down in history
E very day saying *do'h!*
N ew things are done
E ven the boring and the fun
R ightfully the to be best generation
A lthough you might have guessed.
T here is no better generation yet
I s that right you might ask?
O f course we say
N othing's better than my generation.

Ananta Handley (11)
Caldew School

When I Was Born

When I was born my mum and dad said to me,
You are the most precious baby that there will ever be,
When I grew up a bit my mum and dad said to me,
Stick in at school and maybe you could be:
A fireman, a policeman or a farmer too,
An architect, a builder or anything you want to.
But whatever I do, I know who I am
I am Adam Davidson, that's who I am.

Adam Davidson (11)
Caldew School

My Generation

By the time you get old
You can't do as many fun things
So it's boring being old
When you are young you can
Party all night long

My generation
My generation, baby

My generation was fun when I
Was young
I had fun when I was young
Still I can have fun just not
As much

Even though you are old you can
Still do fun things in life.

Abigail Strong (11)
Caldew School

My Generation

My generation are not all yobs
Some will grow up to have good jobs
Some of them might be bad
But not nearly as bad as my dad.

My generation raises cash
By doing the Great North dash
It's not their fault that they are bad
It's the fault of their mum and dad.

So there it is my generation
It's one of the best in the nation!

Chris Gracey (12)
Caldew School

My Generation

Our generation is the best,
With so many individual types of kids.
The worst are the nerds,
Who sit and watch birds.
And they actually like work,
At the library they will lurk.
Chavs on bikes with hoodies on,
Walls full of graffiti that they have drawn.
They always hang around MaccyD's
Listnin' to tunes by random MCs.
The wannabe WAGs wanna be posh,
But they are so not in the dosh.
They buy WAGs' perfume and copy their hair
They wanna marry a millionaire.
The girly girls are also there,
Always got perfect hair.
They totally love the colour pink,
And necklaces with golden links.
The scary black goths have arrived,
They don't really wanna survive.
Wearing black and being depressed,
Walking through town like they're possessed.
And then there's the criticism we get,
By people who we haven't even met.
They're old wrinkled and have grey hair,
They see us, tut and prejudge us.
And one thing they never seem to get is that,
Different groups like goths and chavs,
Will never ever get along.
But we're still a generation,
That totally rules,
The nineties' kids,
Are oh so cool . . . !

Helen Brown (12)
Caldew School

My Generation

M y generation is -
Y ob spraypainting vandals,

G angs hang on street corners,
E nemies fight all night,
N o more old school,
E ggs on people's houses and cars,
R ules are there to be broken,
A ttack old ladies in the street,
T errorising people all through the night,
I want my own space,
O ld people always complaining,
N o effective ASBOs.

Jon Smith (12)
Caldew School

My Generation

M y generation is . . .
Y obs and jobs

G angs and murders
E nergy and helpfulness
N asty young people
E go and phones
R iots and fights
A wesome things to do
T errific games for gadgets
I nspired by friends
O pportunities and regrets
N ike and Fred Perry.

Ryan Bird (12)
Caldew School

My Generation

What's a chav? I hear you say,
They're lads like me, our
Generation today.

To be a chav,
You must have bling,
To wear the chains, rings and things.

I'm not a goth,
I don't wear black,
I wear Lacoste and Burberry,
Upon my back.

I knock around within a gang,
To prove ourselves,
We do the town,
We hit the clubs, and bars most nights,
And wander home feeling alright.

James Metcalfe (13)
Caldew School

My Generation

Back in my day, we used to play out,
But now it's all changed, and they all just shout.

Back in my day, we used to dress up,
But now it's all changed, and they're all just scruffs.

Back in my day, we used to care,
But now it's all changed, it's all about hair.

Back in my day, we used to help out,
But now it's all changed, what's that all about?

Sam Richards (14)
Caldew School

My Generation

Being young is fantastic,
In the old days it was boring and dull,
Being young is like Christmas Day,
Being young is like getting paid,
Like going to the beach with your bucket and spade.

Old people think we are ASBOs with hoodies,
It makes me feel mad,
They think we wreck everything,
They think we hang out on street corners,
But really we don't.

When old I won't treat people badly,
I will treat old people with respect,
When I'm old I will not judge everyone like one person,
I think young people are cool,
I think old people are just well old.

Luke Andrews (11)
Caldew School

Let Us Shine

It's our time
You won't let us shine
Talkin' about my generation
Takes some concentration

Got to understand we're not all yobs
And we ain't all got those big gobs
Does it matter what we look like
Does it matter if we do a wheelie on a bike?
Does it matter if we get hurt in the crossfire?
Believe it or not you're not our style
Some read books
Don't care about looks

Grandma and grandad leave us alone
We don't like your tone
You must put us down
Not all of us mess around and go to town.
Boyfriends and girlfriends so confusing
You make our generation feel as if we're losing
You're just mean
Carry on staring.

Do you remember you used to be us?
Did you forget that special buzz?
Go away you're had your time
Now let me have mine.

Emily Clarke (12)
Caldew School

My Generation

My generation
Teenage mums and dads.
My generation
Hooligans and chavs.
My generation
Yobs and druggies.
My generation
Vandals and thugs.
My generation
Thick and riffraff.
My generation
Spoilt and bullies.
My generation
MSN and mobiles.
My generation
Plain and scruffy.
My generation
Gangsters and hoodies.
My generation
Annoying and underage sex.
My generation
iPods and PlayStations.
My generation
Make-up and slobs.
My generation
Covers all of this.
My generation
Is an abyss.

Victoria Neil (15)
Caldew School

What Do We Care?

They're old and wrinkly,
What do they know,
All things different,
We like to have a go.

Perms and bonnets,
Are a thing of the past,
Mobiles, iPods and laptops,
Won't last.

Mummy and Daddy,
With pocket full of cash,
You're spoilt rotten,
Grannies' tongues will lash.

Junk food and drink,
What do we care,
They all shout,
You're a right mardy mare.

Bags, tags, lads and fags,
All a bonus to make Mum mad,
She thinks we're bad,
So we rebel,
What do we care?
Just go to hell!

Charlotte James (14)
Caldew School

My Generation

Wake up grandma,
I'm here to say.
That things aren't the same,
As they were in your day.

We pierce our ears,
Noses and lips,
We wear make-up and hoodies,
And jeans on our hips.

We need our laptops,
And plasma TVs,
Mobile phones, Game Boys,
iPods and mp3s.

So go to sleep Grandma,
That's all I have to say.
Because things aren't the same,
As they were in your day.

Harriet Coulthard (14)
Caldew School

My Generation

My generation has so many things
Gadgets, techno and plenty of bling.

My generation has sleek mobile phones
And the constant sound of crazy ringtones.

My generation has satellite TV
But people still suffer from HIV.

My generation has high powered cars
And long stretch limos to ferry the stars.

My generation has smart high street shops
Where my friends and I can shop till we drop.

My generation are conscious of fashion
We wear our clothes with pride and a passion.

My generation is full of celebs
Who party all night whilst we're in our beds.

My generation has teenagers on show
With tattoos and piercings from head to toe.

My generation has a difficult life
With teenage hoodies who carry a knife.

My generation has lovely, sweet grannies
Who hide everything in nooks and crannies.

My generation, we have so much
But for many people this is not enough.

Laura Webster (14)
Caldew School

My Generation

Hoodies and make-up,
Drugs and drink.
Mugging and crime,
That's all they think.

Skirts and fashion,
Lipgloss and curls,
Unhealthy lives,
And pregnant girls.

Junk food and loud tunes
It'll go out of fashion soon.
Text talk and slang,
Celebrities and gangs.

Emos and chavs,
What difference do they have?
Piercings and tattoos,
It'll all change soon.

Corinne Irving (14)
Caldew School

My Generation

They think we make trouble,
But really we don't.

Piercings everywhere,
But do we really care?

We drink and we smoke,
They think we're a joke.

Straighteners and make-up,
Our morning routine.

Mobiles in our hands
Headphones in our ears.

Fashionable clothes all over our bodies,
Always posing in the mirror.

We have TVs and laptops of our own,
We always find time to stop and moan.

We scream and we shout,
When everyone's about.

Spoilt rotten,
The old days forgotten.

Eleanor Preston (14)
Caldew School

Changes

6-year-old no care in the world
16-year-old hair perfectly curled
6-year-old a grazed knee
16-year-old hurt by he

30 now getting old
30 now feel like mould

6-year-old played with my toys
16-year-old kissed all the boys
6-year-old looking sweet
16-year-old feeling the heat

30 now husband and house
30 now quiet as a mouse

6-year-old ate fish fingers
16-year-old fancied them singers
6-year-old drank some Coke
16-year-old began to smoke

30 now settled down
30 now no going to town

6-year-old danced to Spice Girls
16-year-old wanted diamonds and pearls
6-year-old played on the park
16-year-old carved my name in the bark

Things were so different between six and sixteen
Being 30 is not so mean
Before I know it I'll be sixty-one
All of a sudden life's passed and gone.

Becca Lamb (16)
Caldew School

My Generation

G eneration
E ducation
N ot trying to cause a big sensation
E njoyment high
R ats in the town
A nd we're just trying to get around
T ry and put us down
I t's my generation
O ut all night
N ot getting old.

Martin Hall (12)
Caldew School

Fibreglass Tavern

Evening now and crisp, cutting, cool.
The tavern windows glow gaily,
Alluring passers in the cold street.
Routledge, sixty-seven and regular
Sits and sips his pint; it's a bitter night.

Miles and years apart crisp, cutting, cool
Starlight is refracted through fibreglass.
A bus shelter under which Malcolm, fourteen,
Huddles, hunched next to the smoking Freya -
Nick has gone for bottles of booze.

The frothing subsides to a warm amber,
Routledge admires the smooth taste, tickling,
Sliding silkily - senses enveloped.
'A slight toffee character - a blend
Of malts, two strains of yeast and choice hops.'

Nick pours the liquor into plastics
To avoid hassle from prying cops.
None have the stomachs for evil spirits which
Descend so violently on virgin tongues.
But Malcolm wants a piss-up.

Perhaps always a stained white satin but not
Ravaged so mindlessly as These Days.
Where there is freedom the young ones
Hang over the cliff edge, naively.
No care or fear of gastric lavage as yet.

Routledge leaves leisurely at eleven.
Rosy tavern windows glow gaily
Through the cloudless night air.

Meanwhile Malcolm swears and spits at Nick.
Freya lies askew on the black road, paralytic.

Timothy Cottingham (17)
Caldew School

My Generation

My generation is . . .

CDs not tapes
DVDs not videos
Mobiles not bricks
Heels not platforms

My generation is . . .
Vodka not tea
£20 not £2
Punches not parties
Make-up not dirt

My generation is . . .

Amy Dawes (13)
Caldew School

My Generation Is . . .

My generation is very hi-tech
My generation is very fun

My generation is better than yours
My generation is easy with chores

My generation is full of laptops
My generation is full of iPods

My generation is simply the best
My generation is better than the rest.

My generation is . . . my generation.

Allicia Corry (12)
Caldew School

My Generation!

My generation is different,
It is more modern to the older generation,
These are a few of our favourite things,
Texting and chatting all day,
Watching TV and playing games,
Going on our phone and chilling with our mates,
Curling and straightening our hair is what we do best,
Getting new pets and learning new things,
Having a laugh and a drink,
These are things from our generation.

Generation,
Generation,
They are all different.

Our generation is different,
It is older to the new generation,
These are a few of our favourite things,
Hunting and chasing,
Knocking and gnashing.
Boxing and fighting,
Enjoying ourselves in the cheapest way,
Unlike today,
These are things from our generation.

Generation,
Generation,
They are all different.

Angharad Percival (12)
Caldew School

My Generation

My generation is an age of technology
With iPods, mp3s and phones
TVs, computers and laptops
PlayStations and gaming

My generation is an age
That is fast moving
With cars, bikes, planes and trains
My generation is the age of technology.

Ben Hodgson (12)
Caldew School

2007

In 2007 we're swearing
Not caring,
We're texting on our phones
Many people taking loans,
Smoking and joking
Wearing chav hats
And the Nike Air Max.

Now we're on computers
And there's lots of looters
We're watching the telly
While stuffing our belly.

Loads of people fighting
It's not really that frightening.

Jamie Foster (12)
Caldew School

My Generation

In our generation;

There are people texting on phones
And people having moans and groans

People staying inside
Because they are too scared to come outside

Young people smoking all the time
And everyone thinks it's fine

People playing on the PlayStation
And everyone praising the nation

Seeing people on their bikes
But soon everyone will be on motorbikes

Everyone swearing
No one caring

Everyone watching telly
And putting food in their belly

People recycling tins and cardboard
Then people going out to fraud

So have a good time
And make your life fine.

Ashleigh Hunter (12)
Caldew School

Boy Racers

Boy racers flying round, won't stop or slow down

All sooped up, cars a-shine, needle bouncing off the red line

Tyres smoking, engine hot, a care for anything they have not

Attention they attract, with their obvious criminal act

The police give chase, which to them is a laugh and a race

There is only one winner, when the police deploy the stinger

The game is over they face the book, the smiles have disappeared
as they have run out of luck.

Matthew Boak (12)
Caldew School

My Generation!

Chocolate and crisps all over my room
My trainer laces wrapped around the broom
Straighteners and hairdryers all in a knot
Mobile phones cost a lot

Television and pink laptops
Jazzy sports cars with flat rooftops
Sweets in a pile on the floor
Maths lessons are such a bore

PlayStations and computers too
Fashionable clothes and bowling, yahoo
Going to the cinema and shopping I do a lot
This season's jewellery is really hot

McDonald's I love, so do my friends
It's all Mum's money so I just have to spend
The Internet I can't live without
My Nintendo DS which is always out

This is a poem about my age group
So go away and jump through a hoop!

Helen Little (12)
Caldew School

My Generation

Plasmas and PlayStations
iPods and CD players
Digital cameras and Sky TV
Mobile phone and telephones
Straighteners and hair dryers
MSN and Internet
Laptop and DVD players
MP3 and MP4
Nintendo Wii and PlayStation 3
Hot tubs and saunas
Trampolines and bouncy castles
Dishwashers and washing machines

That's my generation today!

Danielle Sharpe (12)
Caldew School

Once And Now

Once upon a time I was fit and athletic
Now I am all weak and pathetic

Once my wardrobe was full of tricks
Now my wardrobe is stuffed with sticks

Once they thought me a great japer
Now I sit and read the paper

Once upon a time I went off warring
And now I just sit there snoring

We all get old
And we were all once young
It's part of life.

Matthew Coates (12)
Caldew School

My Generation

Hoodies, iPods, mobile phones, the older generation moans
Alcohol, gangs and lots of drugs, our generation must be thugs!
Indie, bands and skinny jeans this is what our generation means
And the 60s are dead and gone but you still try and hold on.

John McBride (17)
Caldew School

My Generation

CD players and MP3s,
Are what we have in my generation.
Record players and cassettes,
Which would you prefer?

Gangs and hoodies and people like that,
Is who you might see in my generation.
Smart dressed people, nice and friendly,
Which would you prefer?

Lots of homework and detentions,
Is what you get in my generation.
Strict school teachers and the cane.
Which would you prefer?

Lots of fighting and action films,
Are what you see in my generation.
Not much choice in films at all,
Which would you prefer?

Football matches and shopping sprees,
Is what you might do in my generation.
Walks in the park and tandem rides,
Which would you prefer?

Which generation would you prefer?
I'll let you decide.

Alice Simpson (13)
Caldew School

My Generation

My generation
Not the most glamorous by far
It may have technology
With iPods and phones
Computers and laptops
But they cost too much for me

There are rich with too much
And poor with nothing
There are wars and gangs
Guns and chavs
Famine and floods
Destruction and crime

My generation may not be the best
But I would prefer it now
Than in 60 years time
When I'm old and wrinkled
Useless and relentless
But . . .

Not all the old are like that
Some are cool and very fit
Some are interesting
Some are nice
And some may have more control
Than we ever may have.

James Taylor (14)
Caldew School

My Generation

(Sung to tune 'The Pretender' by the Foo Fighters)

You keep us in the dark just because you are older x 2
We show our backbones now
You think you are so big, so big
You think we're buried deep but now, we finally make a stand, against you
Just when you've reached the top, you will find it's only temporary,
Temporary here comes our turn

What if I say we're not like the others
What if I say we're not just another one to fall
It's my generation
What if I say we won't be penetrated

We're coming out the dark
We're gonna come back marching in, to you
Come on and have a go
You are only going to fall, again
And when you think we're gone
You find out that it was temporary, temporary, here we come again

What if I say we're not like the others
What if I say we're not just another one to fall
It's my generation
What if I say we won't be penetrated
We're the voice inside your head, you refuse to hear
We're the hand that'll take you down, bend you to your knees
We are better
Better than you
We're the enemy
We will make sure you don't come back, never, never again
So who are you?
Yeah who are you x 3
You keep us in the dark just 'cause you are older

What if I say we're not like the others
What if I say we're not just another one to fall
It's my generation
What if I say we won't be penetrated

What if I say we're not like the others
What if I saw we're not just another one to fall
It's my generation
What if I say we won't be penetrated

So who are you?
Yeah who are you x 3.

Tim Perry (13)
Caldew School

My Generation

No one ever talks
Unless it's to complain
No one ever is unique
And loves to be the same

The music is all too loud
And always so repetitive
There's never peace and quiet
But so, so many fights

It's always drugs and drink
Your street cred and your ego
No one ever likes to be themselves
Pretending to be all macho

No one ever talks
Unless it's to complain
They're always so grumpy
But maybe I'm just the same.

Philip Watts (13)
Caldew School

Riot

Nothing sounds better than the riot
Nothing feels better than our freedom
Nothing smells better than the burning
Nothing tastes better than victory

Just shut up, we won't give up the fight
Just shut up, it's not all bright lights
Just shut up, it's not partying all night
Just shut up, this just ain't right

Maybe you think it's all easy
Maybe you think that we don't think
Maybe you think we don't even care
Maybe we think that you're not even there

We'll do just fine without you
Young and old just don't mix
Rock 'n' roll, enjoy our youth
I won't watch you look down on us
We'll do just fine without you
We're only having fun!

Jeni Rogers (14)
Caldew School

Generation

I might be young but I feel like I'm old
I am a good guy and I do what I'm told
But still nothing's good enough in this world

This generation is too dull for me
This generation is too old for me
And I'm way too bored.

I want to get away and fly in the sky
I need to see something wide and high
But I'm stuck in this awful place I must not lie

This generation is too dull for me
This generation is too old for me
And I'm way too bored.

Alex Magill (13)
Caldew School

My Generation

When I am old and look back on today,
I'll see a girl who was lucky in every way.
Technology gave me a fantastic life,
With computers and games and all things nice.

This however is my only shame,
And to say it gives me so much pain.
I took for granted what some would cherish,
And while I did this children in Africa perished.

I had a brilliant education,
So when I was older I could have a good occupation.
I read books from trees stripped bare,
I watched horror films to give me a scare.

My mum listened to every word I said,
She tucked me up warm in bed.
I went on holiday to get tanned,
And made sculptures in the sand.

My life was all about how we look,
We put on make-up, spread it on like muck.
Being pressured to be size zero,
Those models were never really my heroes.

In my life I've learned a lot,
But the mistakes I made I never forgot.

Kelly-Louise Harding (13)
Caldew School

My Generation

On our mobile phones all day
Listening to pop, rap, MC Wah-hey
All teenagers care about is fashion
Because it is our passion

There is too much crime on the streets
Teens hanging about in gangs
Violence and evil's everywhere
All teens do is swear, swear, swear

Having to make choices all day long
Whether to do right or wrong
Just look at the teens firing guns
How many more people have to die

This is my generation.

Christian Drake (13)
Caldew School

My Generation

Everyone is different across the nation,
So who are you to judge my generation?

Pierced bodies and multicoloured hair,
High heels, mobiles and fashionable wear.

Ugg boots and make-up an inch thick
Binge drinking and making yourself sick.

Hoodies, knives, drugs and short skirts,
People cutting themselves and getting purposely hurt.

But how about your generation what do you do?
There are things that often make us look down on you.

Coughing and spluttering all the time,
Wrinkly and grey haired and a curved spine.

Unable to walk without a stick,
You sit around feeling constantly sick.

Your false teeth and hearing aid,
And always having to be obeyed.

Sat there all alone in your house,
You can only hear a faint creep of a mouse.

If it wasn't for us what would you do?
Without our care and help for you.

Life has moved on and discovered new things,
I know we're not all perfect with a halo and wings.

However we're not all violent, abusive and bad,
And I bet you're not all lonely, frail and sad.

So don't just judge us by what others do,
First you must look in the mirror at the person staring back at you!

Emma Armstrong (13)
Caldew School

My Generation

Entering the world, coming in with a cry,
No longer a twinkle in my daddy's eye,
Looking back at my generation.

French skipping, hopscotch, marbles and tig,
Chasing the boys, oh, that we did.
Looking back at my generation.

Getting a job, starting to save,
Thinking of the future and being brave,
Looking back at my generation.

Mortgage, marriage, kids and all,
Wondering what I did that for,
Looking back at my generation.

Now old age is creeping so fast,
Just don't know how long I'll last
Looking back at my generation.

I sit here now, less friends, more grief,
This is my life although it is brief
What's now left of my generation?

Rebecca Graham (13)
Caldew School

Soup

Now, please let me apologise to begin with,
It is not to hurt you but to let you know,
As you always say 'don't be so rude',
With all our Internet sites and idiotic songs,
You can't expect us not to rebel, it's tragic!

You can't always make us obey you,
'Get good grades', 'turn that bloody phone off',
Well how about you go to school for me today,
Let's see how you adore the life of us ignorant teenagers,
Enjoy the name calling, ridiculous work and detentions.

We're all tired of your wrinkled faces,
Why don't you just leave us all alone?
We can be responsible and look after ourselves,
Give us a bunch of money and it'll replace you easily,
But just to admit, you do make better soup than us.

Tavia Davies (13)
Caldew School

My Generation: Teens

DVDs, handbags and silver hoop earrings,
Mobiles and iPods, TV and chocolate,
Tracksuits, trainers and the chavs that wear them,
These are the teens, why can't you see!

High heels, boots and tight fitted jeans,
Miniskirts, hot pants and designer labels,
Xbox 360s and lots of junk food,
These are the teens, why can't you see!

Footie, PlayStations, and oversized hoodies,
Money, bling bling and fabulous hair,
Make-up, parties and messing around,
These are the teens, why can't you see!

Chatting, texting and emailing your mates,
Going to town, shopping and slang,
Meeting your pals and living a life,
These are the teens, why can't you see!

Annoying our parents and getting detentions,
Teasing the others especially the teachers,
Some can be bad yet some can be good . . .
These are the teens so . . .

Deal with it!

Emma Dickinson (13)
Caldew School

My Generation War

We line up on the road
Them on one side
Us on the other
And then we fight
This is not a battle of guns or knives
But a battle of words

This is not against other generations
But one between my generation

Although they think we're all best friends
The older generations have got it . . .
Oh so wrong, wrong, wrong
There are all of us
And all of them
Better decide what side you're on

This is not against other generations
But one between my generation

The name of our enemy
Is one you may have guessed
Is one you might have heard of
There are several other names
Yobs, vandals, hoodies or . . .
Chavs!

This is not against other generations
But one between my generation
This is me, my side, my friends
Talkin' 'bout my generation.

Claire Allison (13)
Caldew School

My Generation

MSN, Bebo, email and text
This is what we all do best
People want us to change
But I say no, leave us alone and stay away.

R'n'B, pop, gangster and rap
This is what we do, tap, tap, tap.
They all say shush, turn that racket off
But we say no get lost.

Henri Lloyd, Fred Perry, Bench and more
This is what we have to have
We have to keep with the trend
Or we'll go round the bend.

Why can't they just leave us alone.
We don't bother them, they just moan.
Sometimes I can't believe our generation is this way.
We want it to stay that way.

Amy Dugdale (14)
Caldew School

My Generation

Today we like to sit around,
Not go outside and play,
iPods and mp3s are what we listen to all day.

CDs and DVDs not records and tapes,
Computers, laptops.
Nintendo Wiis take their place.

Everyone's like robots, all sitting in their chairs,
But we know no different,
So no one really cares.

So let's have a party,
Get up out of that chair,
You can't change the past but we can change the future . . .
So boogie like there's no tomorrow!

Jordyn Johnston (13)
Caldew School

My Generation

Welcome to my generation,
Some don't care about education,
The streets are filled with chavs and thugs,
Most of them smoke and deal in drugs.

We can't keep up with technology,
Games, consoles and mp3.
Cameras, iPods, phones galore,
Plasma screens, laptops and many more.

Message alert a text's come through,
Dump your bird before she dumps you.
We stroll round town in twos or threes,
And grab a bite at Maccy D's.

Parents need a helping hand,
When they bury their heads in the sand.
The bills keep flying through the door,
And they can't take it anymore.

Trying to keep up with the latest trends,
Buying clothes to impress our friends.
Designer labels aren't worth the price,
Half of them don't even look that nice.

David Beckham and his plastic wife,
Living the dream in their over-paid life.
They're earning a fortune unlike most,
For kicking a ball between two posts.

In Iraq there's lots of wars,
Terrorists fighting and breaking laws.
People killing and people dying,
Families hurting and families crying.

Good or bad life is fun,
I'll miss it when my time is done.
Although global warming is a massive threat,
My generation is not done yet!

Andy Butcher (14)
Caldew School

My Generation

My generation is the best
We have mobile phones and iPods
And labradoodle dogs

My generation is the best
We have DVDs and flatscreens
And fancy coloured jeans

My generation is OK
We eat too much food
To the telly we are glued

My generation is OK
Computer games and laptops
And lots and lots of shops

My generation is bad
Teenagers that smoke
And too much fizzy Coke

My generation is bad
Burning up the earth
Treating it for what it's not worth

My generation, my generation
Let's all have a big celebration.

Jack Shannon (13)
Caldew School

Media Is What It's All About!

Media is what it's all about,
It tells us all the goss,
In Sugar, Heat, Bliss and Shout,
Where you hear about Kate Moss!

You get the fashion update,
To find the look for you,
So take some time with your mate,
Deciding on a shoe!

It dives into the world of sport,
Highlighting the matches and much, much more,
Commenting on those been bought,
Making more money than ever before!

Channels 1, 2, 3, 4, 5,
Cable, Satellite, Freeview and Sky,
TV is what keeps me alive,
It's time to turn the TV off, goodbye!

Laura Potts (13)
Caldew School

My Generation

We are not what they were, we are much better
But they're older and will challenge our intelligence . . .

So we like to prove to them we are not all as stupid as we look.

They always tell us, 'It's not what other people think of you,
it's what you think that matters.'
Oops! We get detentions for throwing pens, 'You look like a right idiot
now that will look bad on your record. And everyone will think you're
a bad influence'
What happened to the words of wisdom?

Hoodies and ASBOs outside the corner shop, they'll look out their
windows and say, 'I wish they would go away, silly little wasters.'
But we'll turn around and say, 'Are you OK love, do you need a hand
across the road?'

Bet they never saw that coming.
Stereotyping, it's awful these days! If they saw someone
in a black school uniform they would instantly think, *oh gosh,
why are they all goths?*

Or a skinny girl with long blonde hair and rosy cheeks.
'Oh gosh, she's anorexic!'

Or a boy on his way to golf practice in his sports clothing.
'Oh dear, they're all 'chavs' nowadays!'

Is that what they really think of us? Surely not?

And if the tables turned it wouldn't be the same.
They can criticise us and we think nothing of it,
but if we were to do the same, then we're 'Age-ist'.

We'll stay out late, until it's dark and so they worry for a while
But then we'll turn around and say 'Well, nothing bad happened, did it?'

We'll get into arguments as most people do
But then we'll turn around and turn the music so loud . . .

That we can't hear their insults.

'Have some respect for your elders!' they say. And we reply, 'Have
some respect for your youngers please.'

Jaki Watt (14)
Caldew School

My Generation Poem

Have fun while you can, it doesn't last long.
Shopping with your friends,
And putting make-up on.

Have fun while you can, it doesn't last long.
Watching many movies
Like King Kong.

Have fun while you can, it doesn't last long.
Wearing skinny jeans,
And using hot hair tongs.

Have fun while you can, it doesn't last long
Going to many parties
Singing lots of songs.

Have fun while you can, it doesn't last long.
Because when you get old,
Your generation is gone.

Shelley Teasdale (13)
Caldew School

Succession

Winds rage across the moorland prominence
And the gnarled oak takes
A long, slow, deep breath
And stands sturdy.
Spring hesitates on the horizon,
Waiting for his consent.
A new generation is ready,
Forming in the shadows.
We are no longer the new, we are the old.
The never-ending circle is once again turning.
I played here when I was young,
When I was the new.
And now as I stand here with my small child
I feel rooted to the ground.
I see through the tree,
Watch my grandmother, great grandmother
Bringing the next generation,
The new buds of our fortune,
Bursting with fresh ideas, a new life
A new generation.

Bethan Daltrey (16)
Caldew School

My Generation

Chavs,
Grebs,
Goths,
Celebs,
Size zero,
Fashion hero,
Hoodies,
Fast food,
Swearing,
Rude,
Always dissin',
Manners missin',
MySpace,
Bebo,
ASBO,
Emo,
That's what you think of us,
Could you be wrong?

Lauren Coulthard (12)
Caldew School

I Once Was Old

I once was young but now I am old.
I now sit alone, on my own, in the cold.
I dream of the records when I used to dance,
The jewellery, the ballgowns put me in a trance.
The make-up, the slippers,
The girls and the boys,
Those young little nippers,
Those old fashioned toys.
When I laughed, when I twirled,
When I danced all night.
When I giggled my way to the earliest light.
I thought my life would never change,
But then my plans were rearranged.
Because now I am old, crippled and grey
I have nothing to do but stare all day.
Stare at the world as it passes me by,
As a new generation is now on the rise.
Everything's changed, everything's new,
I want to go back, and so would you.

Georgina Goddard (16)
Caldew School

A Doll's Life Or The World's Salvation?

We styled their hair,
We changed their clothes.
We made them happy,
Whatever we chose.

Their life was simple,
Their life was kind.
Love was so easy,
But never so blind.

They were who we wanted to be,
Our hopes and dreams and fantasies.
Barbie and Ken, the perfect pair,
Their life was amazing and always fair.

We dreamed of the good, but never the bad,
The encounters our hearts have never had.
The abuse, the starving, the rapes and murders,
The poverty, the politics, the pain and the pressure.
The aids, the fear, the war and the climate,
The world may be ending, our prayers still unanswered.

Who will save us? Our generation?
Do you really think we could be the world's salvation?
The disgusting, disrespectful, disapproved of sort?
That's what you call us, but that's how you taught.

Show us some love, some respect and some trust.
Then you will see that we have it sussed.
We are the future, we are the power.
Don't make it worse just please go and cower.

We'll restore this world's hope, pride and dignity,
Simply because that's the way it should be.

A doll's life, or the world's salvation?
I sure do know what I'd rather be.
As I am part of this generation,
I am so lucky, as I can be me.

Sarah Penrice (17)
Caldew School

Time After Time

Our generation here and now
Bet you can't beat it you won't know how
Our time is the place to be
Look through our eyes and you will see

The positives of this time
Really do blow the line
Technology being the main component
To bring about our atonement
The iPod changing our musical mind
The computer of an intellectual kind
The technological change will never cease
Whereas our generation will decrease
Phones, music, computers, television
Are you in or out make your decision

Although there's a downside to growing right now
All this crime but we don't know how
What has caused us to be this way
And is it how we will stay?
Why should we strike so much fear
Only by us being here
People are so quick to judge
We all aren't like that don't begrudge
Maybe it's changed from years ago
It can't be helped, we don't move slow
We may be young so our minds aren't set
But the social trends you won't forget
Chav, greebo, goth, nerd
But we aren't all one big herd
So break it down and you will see
That you cannot stereotype me.

Katie Walker & Francesca Patterson (16)
Caldew School

Generations On And On

Generation has now become
Such a strange sensation.
Old has now become new
And has led us through.

Talking about my generation.

People grow with the flow
Then become old and go.
We leave our homes
And only talk on phones.

Talking about my generation.

We buy homes and get jobs
We have kids, hoping they won't be yobs.
Then they grow and move on
Beginning the cycle to go on and on.

Jodie Foster (16)
Caldew School

Today

Chavs on street corners
Grebos in parks
Pants tucked inside socks
Jeans trailing on the ground.
People getting arrested
For drinking and drugs
Spray-painting and skating
That's all they do.
Whatever happened to the good old days
When we all dressed the same
And did things the same?

Peter Allison (12)
Caldew School

My Generation

Playing on the beach when I was two
I didn't really know who was who
Going to my gran's house looking in her old eyes
Smelling the smell of old people
I didn't realise, that that would be me in years to come

Here I am sitting in my chair
Waiting on a visit from my dear grandson
What does he do when he comes in,
But looks in my old eyes, with great surprise.

The great circle of life goes on!

Shannon Bell (12)
Caldew School

Through The Eyes Of A Fairy Tale Character

What would it be like to be a fairy tale character?
How do they live in a book?
We can hardly ever arrest a bad guy,
No matter how hard we look!

Cinderella ended up happy,
Even though she started out sad,
In real life there are no seven dwarves,
Just little kids that drive you mad!

But if you think really hard,
You may find something the same:
No matter whether you're real or not,
You cannot always find fame!

Lauren Foskett (11)
St Joseph's Catholic High School, Business & Enterprise College, Workington

What Am I?

What am I? Something of everyday life,
Quite big with many people most young,
At night empty, in the morning flooded,
Weekdays learning, weekends away,
So what am I? Not much just a part of life.

Mathew Poole (11)
St Joseph's Catholic High School, Business & Enterprise College, Workington

Through The Eyes Of A Guinea Pig

My name is Buttons,
I have left my brothers and sisters
To come and live here with my best friend, Hannah
I live in my own cage and really enjoy the space.

My typical day is cool, as you will see,
Hannah comes with water, she also feeds me
I have greens and nutrients which are very, very yummy.

I sunbathe, nibble and enjoy the grass all day,
I am happy where I am and that's all I can say.

My life as a guinea pig is excellent
And now you know why.

Hannah Scott (11)
St Joseph's Catholic High School, Business & Enterprise College, Workington

Fear Vs Bravery

Fear
One word
One meaning!

A teenage girl bullied for 2 years realises that words really do cut deep.
A group of people beat a boy of 12 to death.
A young girl smokes her first cigarette.
A group of boys shout, 'Ugly' to a girl working down the road
A collection for HIV and AIDs is sent round, you ignore it?

Bravery
One word
Many meanings!

A terminally ill cancer sufferer stands up in front of thousands to
discuss her disease, begging for change.
A firefighter dies in a fire saving a young girl, she lives.
A girl of only 13 finds out she is pregnant and keeps the baby.
A young couple go to Africa on honeymoon, to save HIV sufferers.
A woman in Bangladesh works for 20 hours a day to feed
                                                                her starving family.
A five year old boy picks up a friend in the playground.
A teenager stands up to their tormentors.

Bravery, the opposite of fear. Standing up for what is right
and true no matter what stands in the way.

Fighting to within an inch of your life for what you can do
to make this a better place . . . for others.

Kirsty Wright (15)
St Joseph's Catholic High School, Business & Enterprise College, Workington

You May Shout

You may shout abuse like 'fat' at us,
But you don't know what that statement could do.
You could cause somebody to kill themselves just because
You have no idea what it's like
In a way I hope you get anorexia,
Then you would understand
Understand how much you can screw someone up with comments
                                                      like that.

Friends huh?
I don't call us friends,
Threatening to go to the school counsellors or my parents
I told you to stay out of it.
I'm fine, I'm in control.
Unaware of how I looked to others
People telling me I looked 'really ill'
This frustrated me, so I would starve for longer
I had officially lost control.
You say to me I'm pathetic
Just seeking attention
That I'm sick, idiotic
Being thin is the most important thing to me
I feel extremely guilty every time I eat.
Food is my enemy
But it's not just mine.
'Nothing tastes as good as thin feels.'

Abbie Martin (15)
St Joseph's Catholic High School, Business & Enterprise College, Workington

The World Around Me

The world around me is colourful and bright.
The world around me comes alive at night.
The trees around me stand tall.
The trees around me leaves fall.
The people around me laugh and talk.
The people around me run and walk.
The birds around me sing their song.
The birds around me fly along.
The children around me giggle and play.
The children around me come out in the day.
The world around me is different but special.

Sarah Williamson (13)
St Joseph's Catholic High School, Business & Enterprise College, Workington

I Am A Bench

I am a bench look at me.
I am a bench can't you see.
I sit in the park all day and night
You can always spot me because my colour is bright.
I get sat on by skinny people, fat people and tall.
Lazy people, chubby people and even small.
Some of the people that sit on me.
Usually drink a cup of tea.
But when they spill it is a pain.
Because it dries up and leaves a stain.
And even once in the middle of the night
I got a big shock of my life.
This lad who was drunk came up and slept on me.
I was so in shock he should have known.
I'm in a park that isn't his home.
When he was gone other people came and went
Then I suddenly realised my leg was bent.
After a few more weeks it finally broke
I had to wait till someone spoke.
They told some men how I was damaged.
But luckily they took me and they did manage
When I was put back the children did see
That I was new and bright as could be.
So they all came and wrote on me all day
I wasn't happy they will pay.
When other people saw what the kids had done
I got moved into another park which was nicer and fun.
So now I'm a happy bench look at me.
People treat me with respect can't you see.

Jessica Lee (12)
St Joseph's Catholic High School, Business & Enterprise College, Workington

The Game Of My Lifetime

I'm waiting for England to sing
For their loyal queen and king.
All the opponents can smell is fear
As the match is coming near.
The players are cheering me on
As the hope for the opponents is gone.
Coming through the tunnel of fear
England fans are singing and that's all I can hear.
We have just kicked off the match
And the goalkeeper makes an unbelievable catch.
As I am coming near to the goal
I see in my mind being next to Andy Cole.
I make a wonderfully great pass
Across that very short green grass.
I pass to my mate, best mate Joel
And I get a pass back, from Joel and *goal!*

Karl Monkhouse (13)
St Joseph's Catholic High School, Business & Enterprise College, Workington

Meaning Of Life

Do we have a world,
Where it is right for us,
We live until we die,
And that is the end of that.

We go around a corner,
We go around a bend,
We don't know where we are
Until we reach the end.

We have plenty of money,
We go into a shop,
We come out broke,
And we don't know what we got.

If we live our lives now,
Like we do all the time,
We'd better sort out,
Our adult life in time.

Jordan Cameron (13)
St Joseph's Catholic High School, Business & Enterprise College, Workington

Through The Eyes Of A Bride

As I wake up on this winter's day,
I will no longer have the same surname,
Oh I wish I wish to not rain,
Or it will just be a pain.
I get my hair done with long blonde curls,
As my bridesmaids are putting on their pearls.
I'm nervous to hell but it won't matter,
Because my dreams of a bride will not shatter,
I put on my white dress and give a smile,
My mum has been waiting for this for a while,
She's crying with happiness what I expect,
Because I haven't been a reject.

As I leave the house all ready to go,
I am ready to put on a big show.
I get into the limo and it's all bright,
My dress has a long train and height,
We head for the church, my belly is hurting,
As the people are alerting.
I stand ready to go with my father in my hands,
Then down the aisle I land,
I see my dreams next to me,
As I say I do, as he sees me,
He replies with the same,
Then I kiss him again and again,
Down the aisle we go down,
Husband and wife! It's a good sound!

We get to the reception I'm so excited,
With the picture I unlighted,
Then I sit down and then comes the speech,
With the best man standing up as he screeched,
My husband says a few words,
Then to the cake like herds.

Then the end of the night we had our dance,
Well we had a good chance,
Now there you go, there's my wedding day,
That is all I have to say.

Becky McQuire (14)
St Joseph's Catholic High School, Business & Enterprise College, Workington

The Meaning Of Life

The meaning of life,
Is to live every day worthwhile,
Never let anyone or thing get in the way of that,
To bring up offspring and care and love them so,
To never neglect your own,
Never give up hope that your dream will come true,
Never wish to grow up too soon,
Always believe in yourself and never let others down.

Shannon Jennings (12)
St Joseph's Catholic High School, Business & Enterprise College, Workington

My Generation

Third world people locked away in poverty
While we are let go and set free.

As we eat our morning toast
Third world people are like ghosts.

As we pass by every day
They watch their dreams wash away.

So come on let's change this day by day
Let's help those people and change our ways.

Third world people here we go,
We've come to help you, now say hello.

Now I've talked 'bout my generation
Let's help those people in the third world nations!

Daniel Grierson (12)
St Joseph's Catholic High School, Business & Enterprise College, Workington

Talking About My Generation

Through the window of today
The view is quite jumbled
There is poverty and war
And the advantage of food and water

Happiness and hope
Is all we really need
If we could only share this light and
Warmth with the people who are in need

Recycling paper, plastic and cans
Is all we need to do
To put this planet back in shape
And start the world anew

Car fumes are the worst
It's all we really need
To pollute the air we breathe
Progress and selfishness are now our creed.

Megan Davy (12)
St Joseph's Catholic High School, Business & Enterprise College, Workington

What Am I?

I'm as lifeless as a door
I sway in the wind
With an autumn breeze
Then I lose leaves
And gain them in the spring

What am I?

I'm a tree.

I'm small and white
I scamper on the floor
I'm called Jerry in a TV show
I come through a gap
I like to have cheese
And I'd love a nap.

What am I?

I'm a mouse.

Lewis Pettit (13)
St Joseph's Catholic High School, Business & Enterprise College, Workington

Through The Eyes Of A Window

I'm a window
Only an old school window
But I'm proud to be a window
Because through St Joseph's school I have seen
More than anyone else ever did.

I love the way I am
I love the way I'm built
I love my house
I love my English classroom.

I've learned a lot of the past ten years:
I have seen fights; I have seen a teacher romancing;
I have seen tears dropping out of their eyes
But I have lived the most lovely life.

Sometimes it has been a funny day
Sometimes I have nearly cried
Sometimes we all had a lovely laugh
When Ms or Sir had shouted a name the wrong way,
When her or his laptop forgot to work.

I know that windows cannot die
But when a teacher or a student leaves a school,
I feel like I am going to die
But I can still say that I have the most lovely life.

Indre Arbataviciute (12)
St Joseph's Catholic High School, Business & Enterprise College, Workington

Workington

The weather round here is wet
But the odd day is dry
Normally it's raining
Like Heaven starting to cry

There's a lot to do round here
Like skate and go to town
Cinema, gigs and all the rest
The land is up and down

There's the skatepark
Monroe's (that's the best)
HMV
Not much to detest

So come to Workington
And you will see
There's a lot to do
That will make you happy!

James Wilson (13)
St Joseph's Catholic High School, Business & Enterprise College, Workington

What Am I?

I have no legs but I lay eggs,
I slither fast through the grass,
I cannot blink to be honest I don't stink,
I shed my skin and when I eat I'm not thin,
I sometimes have venom, I sometimes don't,

But what am I?

Jacob Holloway (12)
St Joseph's Catholic High School, Business & Enterprise College, Workington

The Horse Race

At the ring of the bell one horse fell,
But the others started the race.
A bay horse soon took the lead,
But fell back to the rear of the ride,
For a thoroughbred he did lack.
The horses stayed closely bunched.

Then a chestnut soon took the lead
At a very fast speed,
He stayed in the lead without much of a challenge,
And raced to the wire,
With the speed of fire,
And proved he was the winner in the roses on the Derby day.

Lauren Dmytrowski (12)
St Joseph's Catholic High School, Business & Enterprise College, Workington

Through The Eyes Of A Window

I love the way I am built
I love how I open and close,
And how I let a breeze in.

I love having all the attention,
I love to see students in detentions,
And to hear teachers in discussions.

I love that I am made of glass,
And that I have a handle.
I love that I can come in different shapes and sizes.

I love it when someone opens me when they are hot,
And I love it when they close me if they are cold.

I love the way I am hidden behind curtains and blinds.
I love being a window.
I love to let a beautiful smell in but not out
I don't like to let flies in,
But I love to let them out.
I hate to let smoke in,
But I love to let it out.

Sometimes I am locked but I am mainly unlocked.
But I think I'm a window and I think I am right!

Laura Gray (13)
St Joseph's Catholic High School, Business & Enterprise College, Workington

Rabbits

I know I may be a rabbit,
But I have this weird habit.
Is that I talk all day,
That's what they say.

I love my little house,
That I share with a mouse.
My name is Sunny,
Which I think is nice for a bunny.

All my friends,
Have cool trends.
I do too,
How about you?

My fur is grey,
And it looks nice during the day.
My mum's called Toffee,
And my dad is called Coffee.

I live in the grass,
Which people pass.
We have a good time,
Until it's time to dine.

Sophie McCullock (12)
St Joseph's Catholic High School, Business & Enterprise College, Workington

Generation

G eneral people have poor attitude,
E very person has feelings and thoughts,
N ever be aggressive because they will be back,
E ven animals have rights,
R emember to treat people like you would like to be treated,
A lways look after things you've got,
T ell people good news not bad news,
I f you are happy tell people you are happy,
O ne Earth so I look after it,
N ever hurt yourself you might hurt others.

Matthew Johnson (12)
St Joseph's Catholic High School, Business & Enterprise College, Workington

If I Could Change Anything!

If I could change anything in the world,
I would change hardly anything,
Because I love
The plants, I love the trees, I love the summer breeze.

If I had to change anything in the world,
I would change hardly anything,
Because I love
The autumn leaves pittering on my mam and dad's car.

If I could change anything in the world,
I would change hardly anything,
Because I love
The winter snowflakes falling to the ground.

If I could change anything in the world,
I would change hardly anything,
Because I love
The spring clean out the dust tickling my nose.

If I could change anything in the world,
I would change hardly anything,
But the one thing I would change
The creepy-crawlies crawling around my house at . . .
Night.

Rebekah Curwen (12)
St Joseph's Catholic High School, Business & Enterprise College, Workington

My Poem

If there's anything in the world that I
Could change it would be racism.

If there's another thing in the world that I
Could change it would be crime.

If there's another thing in the world that I
Could change it would be terrorists.

If there's another thing in the world that I
Could change it would be animal cruelty.

If there's another thing in the world that I
Could change it would be child cruelty.

Katie Jackson (12)
St Joseph's Catholic High School, Business & Enterprise College, Workington

Our Generation

Our generation feels small but big.
Our generation full of gigs.
Our generation's technology full.
Our generation's out to pull.

Technology is all around us.
Technology's the one that gets us through.
Technology's in everyday life.
Technology is the one I like.

Jamie Graham (13)
St Joseph's Catholic High School, Business & Enterprise College, Workington

New School

The days have come
For me to see my school,
If I survive a day or two

Harder work has come today
Through my next 5 years
At this school,
To enjoy every second
While it lasts

Even if it's the high school dance
But now it's the trials,
For the football team.

Ashley Dixon (11)
St Joseph's Catholic High School, Business & Enterprise College, Workington

Futurama

Cars hovering,
Robots working,
That's what I think the future will be like.

Fancy gadgets to help you in your everyday lives.
Including auto drive.

Police handling new made cities with help from their new guns.
No crime and no thieves because they've been pelted
                                            by the auto police.

No war and no world's end that's what I think the future will be like.

Ryan Allenby (11)
St Joseph's Catholic High School, Business & Enterprise College, Workington

The Day I Started Secondary School

The day I started secondary school,
My heart and head were pounding,
The pages of my file flew out,
As I'd broke its red binding.

The day I started secondary school,
So many teachers and classes,
The tiny door was tightly crammed,
My best friend broke her glasses.

The day I started secondary school,
Trying to blend with the rest,
Every teacher that I met,
Said always do your best.

Natasha Oldale (11)
St Joseph's Catholic High School, Business & Enterprise College, Workington

In My Future World

In my future world I would like to say
For everyone to come and play.

In my future world I would like to say
The robots should do all the work during the day.

In my future world I would like to say
That for food and water you shouldn't pay.

In my future world I would like to say,
That everyone should be kind and gay.

This is my future which I would like to stay.

Rebecca Doyle (11)
St Joseph's Catholic High School, Business & Enterprise College, Workington

Tree, Tree

I am tall and sometimes small,
I can smell but don't like Hell,
Haven't you heard I am a tree
That girl who told you, who had a fat knee.

There is a boy who came to me
And he said in a cryish type of voice:
'I really hurt my knee.' Now all the children come to me.
And tell me their worries, so aren't I a fantastic tree?

Alannah Bateman (11)
St Joseph's Catholic High School, Business & Enterprise College, Workington

Not Real

I am a table
Got gum on me

I get kicked
I feel sick

I get worked on all day long
But when they have gone
I go to sleep with my song.

Charlotte Mary Fee (11)
St Joseph's Catholic High School, Business & Enterprise College, Workington

H$_2$0 A - Ω

I'm just a cloud
Part of the water cycle
But I see a lot
Through my journey
From up in the sky
To down on the ground
Good and bad I see all around

When I'm in the form
Of a mountain stream
Not many trees
Are there, to be seen
Though you can type things
Most trees are cut down
And no one will see that great big noun

Thank you, thank you
For making me clean
I feel good
And you don't get poisoned
Technology's cool
Plus it's going up
Maybe hover scooters out of the muck

Back in the sky
As a fab cloud
I go round and round
Long ago your kind were rubbish.
Now you're quite good I admit
In future times you might be the best
But if you meet aliens you'll be put to the test.

Megan Smeaton (11)
St Joseph's Catholic High School, Business & Enterprise College, Workington

Through The Eyes Of The Homeless

Through the eyes of the homeless,
The long days, the cold days go by,
No friends. No money. No life.
The wind, rain, cold and nowhere to hide.

I smell and I am unwashed,
No job. No money. No clean clothes.
Just me on my own with no warmth,
Unloved; Unhappy; Unclean

Me and my sleeping bag for love,
The laughing; the dirty looks as they walk by;
The faces they pull then I ask for change,
Passing with bags of shopping and food;

Drinking in front of me as if it's funny. I need a drink,
Lucky I get something to eat in a week.
Long, unwashed hair down my face,
The cold in my feet all the time.

Will I get off the streets
Or will I die a nobody?

Jack Wilson (14)
St Joseph's Catholic High School, Business & Enterprise College, Workington

Through The Eyes Of A Horse

I wake up to the same four walls.
I stand up and give myself a shake.
A bit later my owner lets me out.
Into the green spacious fields.
I'm thinking, *great lots of grass to eat.*
Plenty of space to run around.
I start eating away,
Getting ready to go wild.
But no, they come and tack me up.
Take me to the manager.
She gets on me and welts me in the side.
So I start moving,
I do all this exercise.
Then they take all those heavy things off my back.
And put me back into my field.
Yes food.
I haven't got the energy to go wild.
I'll just eat instead.
They come and get me when it gets dark.
Lock me up again and give me a good meal.
I settle down for the night.
Same again next day.
Better get a good sleep.

Becca Clark (13)
St Joseph's Catholic High School, Business & Enterprise College, Workington

Through The Eyes Of A Bird

Through the eyes of the bird
It used to be a beautiful place
Now it has turned into a tip
Usually I can't kip because
Of all the noise and children
Shouting, everyone used to be nice and kind to us
It used to be a nice quiet and funny place
All my mates used to live in all the luscious
Trees that were planted but
The worse this gets is when it is
Winter where I have to fly
I get there it is a perfect place
It is like heaven, you can bathe
In the water of a goal it is like heaven I love it,
It is the best in the world.

Sam Fisher (13)
St Joseph's Catholic High School, Business & Enterprise College, Workington

My Generation

I get up at 7.30
To go to school,
I wrap up warm in the winter
Because it's normally cool.

When I reach school
I chat with my friends,
And see what time,
Together we may spend.

In school I have
Lessons of assorts,
Maths, RE, science
English and sports

The weekend that's
The best
Because I only go home
For a rest

Also through
The week
I spend and spend time
On my piano and guitar

That's my life
Can't you tell?
Isn't my life
Rather swell.

Rebecca Spedding (13)
St Joseph's Catholic High School, Business & Enterprise College, Workington

What Am I?

I am tall
My nickname is a fruit
I can't move
I'm one of the biggest things in the world
People walk all over me every day
What am I?

Ashley Jenkinson (12)
St Joseph's Catholic High School, Business & Enterprise College, Workington

A World Of The Future

I wake up to the same boring household
I go boringly to get my breakfast
I boringly get changed for school and leave
I boringly do my work and boringly come home
Until . . .
The future . . .
When I wake up to a new room . . .
I go to get my breakfast in a cool way . . .
I get changed and leave for school in a cool car . . .
And do all my work and come home in a cool car again . . .
And that is a world of the future.

Katie-Leigh Walton (13)
St Joseph's Catholic High School, Business & Enterprise College, Workington

Through The Eyes Of The Sun

Although I am just a star, I am a star;
I supply life and light to Earth,
Without me nobody would live,
I shine my light upon the darkest places of the solar system.

I will never give up shining my light on those that need it most,
I will never die out,
Only when the light shines out.

Harry Crawshaw (11)
St Joseph's Catholic High School, Business & Enterprise College, Workington

Through The Eyes Of A Singer . . .

Through the eyes of a singer,
Lights beam at you on stage,
Fans scream and shout your name,
You sing like a bird and shine like a star.

Through the eyes of a singer.
You sing like never before,
Touch the fans' hands as they scream,
And wave as you go backstage.

Sophie Holding (11)
St Joseph's Catholic High School, Business & Enterprise College, Workington

Through The Eyes Of A Fish

I am a fish
My tail goes swish,
It's so fun for me
Swimming in the deep blue sea.
My friends and I play
Around the ocean all day.
Now we better hurry
And really worry
For the sharks roar
As they sweep across the ocean floor.
Now it's time to go to bed
So I can rest my sleepy head.

Robyn Taylor (11)
St Joseph's Catholic High School, Business & Enterprise College, Workington

People Of The World

Poor people have no money
Rich people have money
Old people are fragile
Youthful people are strong
Homeless people have no home
Home owners have a home:

P is for poor people
E is for enthusiastic people
O is for outstanding people
P is for polite people
L is for lovely people
E is for energetic people.

Mark Clark (11)
St Joseph's Catholic High School, Business & Enterprise College, Workington

Through The Eyes Of Michael Owen

Today's the day!
The day I'm back!
To help Newcastle get back on track.
If we play as a team
And hit a good seam,
There is no reason why
We couldn't reach for the sky.
With Given and Martins and Geremi
Too I'm quite sure we can win a few.
With our front two, Martins and me,
We could knock a couple past Cudicini.

Calum Best (11)
St Joseph's Catholic High School, Business & Enterprise College, Workington

Steven Gerrard

My name is Steven Gerrard
I play for Liverpool
People come to see us play
Because they think we're cool

I am a midfielder
I sometimes score goals
I kick the ball
And try to get between the poles

I like my life
I like it very much
If you work hard enough
You can have a life as such.

Kieran Davies (11)
St Joseph's Catholic High School, Business & Enterprise College, Workington

I'm A Football Player

As the ball goes
Long and fast,
I see it go
Flying past,
I heard my toe
Do an almighty crack,
Which ended up
Really black.

I thought that this
Was going great,
Until Ronaldo
Stepped in place,
As he shot
At the goal
I wanted to be
In the North Pole.

As the ball landed
At my feet,
I saw a fan's face
Glow with heat,
Which at this time
I aimed to score,
And then my luck
Shone once more.

I scored!

Matthew Poole (12)
St Joseph's Catholic High School, Business & Enterprise College, Workington

Through The Eyes Of Steve Irwin

It would have been fun to be Steve Irwin
Having the nickname Croc Hunter
And working with other wild and exotic creatures
Also having a willing team of helpers
And a beautiful park to work in.

Ben Welsh (11)
St Joseph's Catholic High School, Business & Enterprise College, Workington

In The Eyes Of A Leeds Rhinos Supporter!

A little bit of Peacock in our lives
A little bit of Donald down the sides
A little bit of Ellis is what we need
A little bit of Burrow with his speed
A little bit of Webb in defence
A little bit of McGuire he's immense
A little bit of chanting from the fans
A little bit of Sinfield he's our man
A little bit of gossip from the commentator
A little bit of Sculthorpe as the spectator
Leeds and Wigan face each other in a match
After they've kicked the ball they have to catch
It's 30-14 to Leeds at 5 minutes to go
It's Burrow to Webb
To McGuire
To Peacock
And he dives to the try line too low for no one to go
Sinfield has to kick
Tony the manager has to pick
And there's McGuire, he's placed the kick right over the top corner of
the post
And there's the Claxon, no more to go.

Bradley Lawrence (12)
St Joseph's Catholic High School, Business & Enterprise College, Workington

Through The Eyes Of The Sky

I know I have no eyes and I do not have a brain,
But I know one side of the Earth is sunny,
And the other is in the rain.

I feel footballs flying everywhere in England and in France,
And in Australia I can see some children learning to dance.

Over in East Africa the poverty is clear,
Oh, how sad it is to see the people disappear.

Every day more people are lost,
Just because some people won't go to the cost,
Of recycling their rubbish once a week,
They are the people I wish to seek.

If you are one of those people,
You could save lives,
By just recycling your rubbish,
It doesn't take much time.

Alicia Teasdale (11)
St Joseph's Catholic High School, Business & Enterprise College, Workington

Pete On The Street

I'm Pete
I live on the street
My parents left me on my feet
And at night people fight
It's hard for me
I'm only three
And no one likes me
I'm not free
Because of poverty.

Daniel Grisdale (12)
St Joseph's Catholic High School, Business & Enterprise College, Workington

Life Today

Life today, I do not know
School and politicians have sunk so low!
While me and my family eating our fill
Meanwhile in Africa people working for food in a mill
I wish all of this starving was at an end
And all of us could help to mend
We have destroyed the world we have made
Hoping someone will come to our aid
I wish in the future our land is secure
And poverty and war, plus many more.
Were gone from our sights
And never more return!

James Jenkins (11)
St Joseph's Catholic High School, Business & Enterprise College, Workington

Big World

I stand here alone in memory of Con,
Born 1935, died 2001,
Winter, spring summer and fall,
Sunny, rainy, I've stood through it all.

Spring is here March, April, May,
Thrushes chirping in a peaceful way,
Buds start to grow in the trees,
The shivering winds turn to a breeze.

Spring to summer, cloud to shine,
Children on the park, everyone's fine,
Old people, young people, rest on my knees,
Flowers all around, butterflies and bees.

September, October, November are the autumn seasons,
This is my favourite time, of that I have no reason,
Autumn leaves are a-falling,
I can hear the winter a-calling.

Winter eventually comes around,
Everyone's at home there's barely a sound,
Twinkling brightly Christmas lights,
Cold, dark, lonely nights.

I am like a statue stood in fear,
I love the world but does the world know I'm here.

Katie Sloan (12)
St Joseph's Catholic High School, Business & Enterprise College, Workington

What Am I?

Summer is here jam-packed full of fun . . .
Children dancing in the sun
As the sun shines so high the sea is a highlight in my eye
I crawl and sleep in the sand and might end up in someone's hand . . .

Sun, sea, sand . . . my perfect day
As the groups of children sing and play
I crawl fast in the sand and I am very small
Can you guess what I am?

1, 2, 3, 4, watch me crawl along the floor
5, 6, 7, 8 lay ice cream sticks straight
All the views of the seaside
But in summer it isn't very easy for me to hide

Have you guessed who I am yet?

Amy Lee (13)
St Joseph's Catholic High School, Business & Enterprise College, Workington

Life As My Friend

Life as a teenager is often very different
Than life as either a child or an adult
It is a rough time with different obstacles to face
And often it seems as if there are many
Many more of them. Let the countdown begin
Through the eyes of a friend
I am small, the world looks down on me
What I've been given
A squeaky voice
But I stand up and take it
My entertainment is my jokes
What keeps me going in school
Sometimes I try to take over
But all goes bad
I use people's words and jokes and info
To get more mates but it gets worse
I will soon grow and my voice will break
This will be the best day
Of my life
Hope it happens soon.

Luke Ellis (13)
St Joseph's Catholic High School, Business & Enterprise College, Workington

Future World

In the future there should be no war
And there should be no deforestation.
In the future there should be no vandalism
Or crime.
In the future everybody should be treated the same
There should be no drugs or fame.
In the future there should be no guns or fighting
And in the future there should be a choice for what the public
Want to do.
In the future there should be no waste of things that could be reused.

Andrew Towers (13)
St Joseph's Catholic High School, Business & Enterprise College, Workington

On The Street

Each day gets longer
And longer on the street,
I am as damp and scruffy as a stray cat in winter that's been living
on the street for 10 years and is on its final legs,
On the street,
Nobody cares,
Nobody notices us we're invisible see,
The people with money ignore us, well most of them do,
I sometimes imagine I was one of these people living in a house,
It's funny how when you have a bed you don't value it,
But that's the one thing that I have that they don't,
I have learned the value of these things like a bed, a house, a family,
So maybe this whole experience is a lesson from God,
And a miracle will happen and tomorrow and I will be in a house again,
I wish.

Jonathon Irving (13)
St Joseph's Catholic High School, Business & Enterprise College, Workington

Mistakes

In your life you make at least one
It leaves you with regret that weighs a ton,
Nobody's perfect not even me
I wasn't thinking neither was she,
First came little Jasmine
Unexpectedly there was Yasmin,
My life was surely over, I had nowhere to turn
After everything I'd been through you'd surely thought I'd learn,
My coat was on and I was ready to go
Yes getting on the plane to Mexico,
Turn over the leaf
Dig in my teeth,
Maybe stay and start up a night club
With my luck it will turn into fight club,
Learn from me and don't be stuck in the mud
Get a job and make your life good.

Kieran McGee (13)
St Joseph's Catholic High School, Business & Enterprise College, Workington

A World For Da Future

A world for da future
Hover cars, invisible robot men
England with nations of every culture
A place in the forest called Da Lions Den
Women and men in Da Lions Den
Of course these people are dead
Robots with special powers called Da Fantastic Ten
A new invention called Da Flaming Bed
An animal as so it seems
With features of a dinosaur
This only eats custard creams
Nothing can kill it apart from a chainsaw
A dogcat, a weird creature
But this will seem da end
Now I conceive a world for da future.

Jordan Swinburne (14)
St Joseph's Catholic High School, Business & Enterprise College, Workington

Through The Eyes Of A Dog

I can't look up, I run a lot, I am furry
Lots of people like me
I bark, I lick, I chase, I growl
I chew, I beg, I play dead
I roll, I eat grass when I am sick
Protect people and other things
I pant a lot when I am hot
I bite sometimes when I am angry
I like food
What am I?
I am a dog.

Tom Fisher (13)
St Joseph's Catholic High School, Business & Enterprise College, Workington

Life As A Fence

Rain drips heavily from the sky, as angry people storm by.

I'm sitting here through day and night,
As there I have only street light.

Through all different weather,
All that passes is a feather.

Lonely soldier I am there,
In the dark,
It's very bare.

It starts to get light,
The sun is bright.

All the children come out to play,
It's a brand new lovely day.

Rebecca Burgess (13)
St Joseph's Catholic High School, Business & Enterprise College, Workington

Where You Bin?

I said hello to my friend Treza
I had breakfast early
I had an apple and a cup of tea from Costa Coffee (more like cost a lot)
Some teenagers bullied me and drew on my top
Someone went to throw rubbish at me and missed
And then he ran down the street
My day was finally over *but* a storm came and blew me down the hill,
Then *C . . . R . . . A . . . S . . . H!*
I hit a house
I broke my legs and cracked my head,
By the way I'm a bin.

Ryan Lea (12)
St Joseph's Catholic High School, Business & Enterprise College, Workington

Theme Park Bench!

I am a bench can't you see,
I am a bench people sit on me,
No one knows who I am.
But I am a bench and my name is Sam.
One quiet day at the theme park a gang of lads came along
With their phones beaming out a song,
The looked horrid I didn't like them,
They sat on me, I wanted to bite them.
They stunk of smoke
And a bit of Coke.
They talked loud and shouted foul words,
They sounded like horrible squawking birds.
At last they stopped the music
I was glad they did I was going to lose it.
The gang stood up, I was glad
Those lads were very bad.
Before they went they pulled a coin from their pocket
And started to carve in his nickname Rocket.
I am a bench can't you see.
I am a bench people sit on me.

Melissa Armstrong (12)
St Joseph's Catholic High School, Business & Enterprise College, Workington

Untitled

I can see you, wherever you may go under my watchful eye
I know the bad people and the good
I have had bad times and good
I know the wanted ones and ones on the run
I can see them but they can't see me
I am nestled behind a tree
I can do the police's dirty work to catch the criminals
Doing their dirty work
You will never cross me
Because I will just catch you on CCTV!

Melanie West (12)
St Joseph's Catholic High School, Business & Enterprise College, Workington

What Am I?

I can see the whole street,
Full of people moving fast on their feet,
People graffitying on the walls,
I can see the children coming home from school,
I can see the birds singing from across the street,
Some people sitting down to have something to eat,
All the cars going past,
Some going slow, some going fast,
As darkness appears people and traffic disappear.

What am I?
A camera.

Carl Robertson (12)
St Joseph's Catholic High School, Business & Enterprise College, Workington

Park Bench

They sit on me, they carve their name,
Yet when I'm scruffy, I'm to blame
They use me as a rubbish bin
Now you tell me, is that a sin?
They bump into me, they scratch my paint,
Is it any wonder I feel faint.
They sit on me with big fat bums
But really they are all my chums.

Rebecca Hunt (12)
St Joseph's Catholic High School, Business & Enterprise College, Workington

How Different Are We From Years Ago

Mobile phones as small as a teabag
iPods that store songs for evermore
Computers to carry, computers for home
Hairdryers, straighteners, curlers and tongs
All this technology
to make our life easier.
Televisions, DVDs, CDs, I could go on and on
How lucky are we today.

In times gone by no such things were heard of
Computers for business
TV to share with the family
Food on ration
Clothes on tic
Luckiness is wonderful.

Melissa Bathgate (12)
St Joseph's Catholic High School, Business & Enterprise College, Workington

What Am I?

I first get touched in a morning
About nine o'clock I'd say.
Most of the people are yawning,
And they do this every day.

Some hands feel rough,
Some hands feel smooth.
Most of them are tough,
Some can't help but groove.

Pushed and pulled I get,
In and out I go.
I haven't fallen off yet,
I will very soon though.

I can come in gold,
Silver, bronze and even chrome.
I am very easy to hold,
You'll find me in every home.

Claire Linford (13)
St Joseph's Catholic High School, Business & Enterprise College, Workington

My Poem!

People sit on me, I'm usually in bedrooms,
I can be in a sofa as well.
People sleep on me,
They sometimes hurt me by jumping on me.
How silly.
Sometimes they invite friends round and sit on me and talk
And sometimes if I'm lucky they share secrets, but that's rare.
People drool on me and that's sick and their feet stink.
And also if they're drunk they will do stuff I can't mention here.
But you may not know.
It's annoying when people wriggle or my springs get broken
Or people throw me away, I get lonely.
But I like getting dressed, it's fun.
They're like dresses but smaller,
But at least I'm still warm.

Chelsea Ritson (12)
St Joseph's Catholic High School, Business & Enterprise College, Workington

Teachers And Lessons

Some teachers are cruel, some teachers are cool,
Some of them make you look like a fool,
Especially the ones that are at our school,
I find most of them cool.

English, maths and science too,
In RE Jesus is a Jew,
Some can be exciting, phew,
But some can be boring too.

Nathan Graham (12)
St Joseph's Catholic High School, Business & Enterprise College, Workington

The World Today

The world today has lots of pollution
People are fighting to find a solution.

Weather is changing on the news
Everybody has their views.

They say there's a hole in the ozone layer,
Caused by things we spray in the air.

We are recycling paper, plastic and tins.
Cutting down on rubbish we put in the bins.

Trying to find a cleaner power.
Using up what we have, hour by hour.

Technology's changing all the time:
Talking to people, while playing online.

Some say talking is a thing of the past.
When sending a text is twice as fast.

Xbox 360, mp3,
Cameras are everywhere watching me.

Watching programmes on TV
Keeping up with reality.

So today things are changing for everyone.
When today is over, tomorrow will come.

Oliver Penn (11)
St Joseph's Catholic High School, Business & Enterprise College, Workington

Mobile Blues

My keys hurt like swollen knees,
She shouts at me without saying please.
Who is this person that bullies me.
She scratches my face,
She leaves me in the dark,
She runs down my battery,
Stop -start
Abusing me like a dog does a bone
All I am is a poor
Mobile phone.

Shannon Stuart (11)
St Joseph's Catholic High School, Business & Enterprise College, Workington

The Page

I am just a page,
People say I have no feelings,
But I do,
I get leaned on all day,
And all night,
It is horrible,
I wish you could feel what I feel,
People write graffiti all over me,
It feels as though people just want to cover me up,
It's horrible,
People swear on me,
People bully on me,
People fold me,
And people throw me,
And every now and again someone writes something,
Beautiful on me and I feel,
Great.

Luke Norman (11)
St Joseph's Catholic High School, Business & Enterprise College, Workington

Forced Out

I was awoken by this sound
My dad went out and found,
Humans cutting down trees,
How scared were we.

My dad said we had to go
No time to be slow,
I was so frightened and terrified
One by one we went.

As fast as we could hop
Then suddenly a tree fell down,
Which caused us all to stop
It made us sad to see.

We had no place to call home
What did we do to them,
For us to have no home?

Jessica Ellis (11)
St Joseph's Catholic High School, Business & Enterprise College, Workington

Abandoned Dog

Why did you abandon me?
Just because I'm not a puppy
You're the one, who took me in,
You should still be loving me.

You're the one that held me
You're the one that loved me.
Now I'm cast aside, so now
I'm trapped and I don't know
When something might attack.

I'm left here alone, day and night
And I don't even get one simple bone
You tied me to this tree
Then left me and you will not come back . . .

Calvin Hodgson (12)
St Joseph's Catholic High School, Business & Enterprise College, Workington

People Think We're . . .

People think we're nasty,
People think we're mean.
People think we're disrespectful and overall not keen.

When you get to meet us,
We are really kind.
When you get to meet us,
We are not so mean
When you get to meet us,
We are not disrespectful and overall we are keen.

People think we're hard to please,
People think we're selfish.
People think we're noisy and overall spend, spend.

When you get to meet us,
We are not hard to please.
When you get to meet us,
We are not so selfish.
When you get to meet us,
We are not so noisy and overall do not spend, spend.

That's what life's like for us.

Courtney Cannell (11)
St Joseph's Catholic High School, Business & Enterprise College, Workington

Our World

This world is sad,
We make it bad.

This land is grey
And wasting away.

This sea is polluted,
Because we do things stupid.

This forest is gone,
Because we do things wrong.

This is our world today!
And it's wasting away!

Naomi Peet (12)
St Joseph's Catholic High School, Business & Enterprise College, Workington

My Life As A Baby

No one can understand me,
I want my tea.
I'm going to scream and shout until they give it me.
Mmm, now my belly's full.
Burp!
But my tummy hurts there's something wrong,
Boy there's such a pong!
There's a warm squidgy thing in my nappy,
I'm going to scream and shout until they sort it out for me.
All squeaky clean now,
Lying snuggled close on my mother's arm,
Cradled snug and safe from harm.
Yawn
Don't you dare put me down,
Or I will show you my big frown,
I won't be a happy baby,
I'll scream and shout until you give in to me!

Rebecca Dolan (12)
St Joseph's Catholic High School, Business & Enterprise College, Workington

Why Have You Done This To Me?

I am a beggar.
Why God did give me
My life like this?
This stupid life.

I am a flying bird.
There is no house for me.
No one likes me.
Why has God done this all?

A long time ago,
A long time ago.
I was rich,
Was in the world.

But now I am poor
Poor in the world, I am
The poor in the world.
Why has he done this?

Long time ago,
Long time ago.
I was a busy
Woman in the world.

But I lost all,
Now I lost all.
Why has God done this?

Why? Why? Why?
Has He done this all?

If I hadn't lost
My family I would be
The luckiest woman
In the world.

But, that's impossible.
Why my dear Lord?
Why have you done this?
To me? Why? Why? Why?

Maria Varghese (12)
St Joseph's Catholic High School, Business & Enterprise College, Workington

Misunderstood Teenagers

Through the eyes of the world
Us teenagers are mean and unreliable
But that's not strictly true
Because teenagers are misunderstood

Teachers often tell teenagers to grow up
And stop being immature
It's life and don't mess it up
Everyone goes through it

That's life so why change that if some
People don't like it
Teachers you have once been a teenager
We all go through it

Although we are mean and immature
All we need is love and care in this world

So why are teenagers so
Misunderstood?

Aiméé Stewart (12)
St Joseph's Catholic High School, Business & Enterprise College, Workington

My Poem

When it comes to write in English our generation is lazy.
Mobile phones are good and new but don't help us
                                        in the English school
The slang in our days is a lot different than the language
                                        our grandparents spoke.
We write using text language.
'What does this all mean?' our grandparents say,
'We didn't use things like this in our day'
The technology has a lot to answer for.
Why can't we do things the old fashioned way?

Andrew Shillito (12)
St Joseph's Catholic High School, Business & Enterprise College, Workington

Our Days In 2007

In our days we have a lot but not as much as you
We have PSP and motor cars but it would be good if we had flying cars
They fly, they swoop and they go fast
Clothes are nice and clean
Lights are chandeliers
You can hang from them with fear
Computers have the Internet that you can search all day
Tellies are big as can be, you can watch telly all day
School is so boring we write, write, write
All I want to do is learn at home, no teachers to tell us off
                                         and give us orders.
Our home is big with lots to do
Too many chores we have to do to make it lovely and clean
But parents get in your way and tell you off for something you didn't do.
There are pets like dogs, cats, rabbits, fish and loads more.

Bethany Lines (12)
St Joseph's Catholic High School, Business & Enterprise College, Workington

Teenager Life In 2007

This is a start of my teenager life.
There are more worries to think now.
The worry I have now is my future.
There is work experience and lessons to choose for next year
to think about.

Oh! My worries, worries, worries.

This is a start of my teenager life.
It is getting boring at school now.
It is boring to have the same lessons for the last 2 years.
All I want is some fun.
Oh! Boring, boring old school.

This is a start of my teenager life.
It is one of my important years of school.
To choose what we need to do.
Oh! School, school, school.

Vivien Ng (12)
St Joseph's Catholic High School, Business & Enterprise College, Workington

The World We Live In

Smoke from factories polluting the air,
Acid rain destroys trees everywhere.
Filthy rubbish on the floor,
Dirty water washes our shore.

Havoc and destruction everywhere,
Kids dying of hunger every day.
Sometimes I just stop to think,
What has happened to this world we live in?
But the answer can only be,
To donate money, and don't give in.

Edi Akpan (11)
St Joseph's Catholic High School, Business & Enterprise College, Workington

Anfield

Every night I feel lonely and cold,
No one to talk to me, I just feel old
The wind swirls around my gigantic walls, and sounds
like a werewolf's call.
But then a shine of light appears,
As the match day comes . . .

Cheers, screams and claps are heard
As the roaring arrives
Myself is then full to the brim
As the silence drops and the whistle is blown.

The ball is moved around inside,
By the players I know so well.
Then an anthem is sung around,
And roars the players on.
Amongst the roars and cheers I hear wails and cries,
As first one team, then the other,
Approach the scoring lines.
Then I burst into a defining cheer,
As we score the winning goal
Hooray!

There goes the whistle
Then everybody leaves and the cheers disappear.
I am lonely for a few more days,
Until the match day comes again.

Liam Cooper (11)
St Joseph's Catholic High School, Business & Enterprise College, Workington

Here He Comes Again

Here he comes again
To play his daily game
Switch me on, grab the controls
It's always the same

Flying round the racing track
Killing aliens in space
I can take him anywhere
And he can win the race

Today he's a great footie player
With lots of brilliant kicks
Tomorrow he could be a skateboarder
Doing dangerous tricks

I am always glad to see him
We really get along
But his man and dad always say
You've been on that too long.

I hear a shout from downstairs
It's time to go for tea
But I know he'll be back to see me
I'm his favourite Xbox 360.

James Taylor (11)
St Joseph's Catholic High School, Business & Enterprise College, Workington

I Say, You Say!

I say,
'Moan, moan, moan, that's all you do.
Nothing you say is ever true.
All we want is to have some fun,
Then you go and moan to our mum!'
You say
'Hoodies and gangs are out for trouble,
All those nasty girls in a huddle,
Talking and laughing and staring at you!'
I say
'It's in your head, it isn't true!
Remember when you were young, only a child,
Well we're the same, we go out but we don't go wild.
We be ourselves, we run about
We talk to our mates, we love going out!'
I say that you
'Moan, moan, moan, that's all you do.'
I say
'Give us a break it isn't true!'

Bethany Burdon (11)
St Joseph's Catholic High School, Business & Enterprise College, Workington

The Meaning

Living in our time,
It's like a dream,
All this technology,
But why are we really here?

God made us His children,
To care for each other,
And make the most of what we have,
Or are we part of a bigger plan?

The oceans, the lakes, the animals,
What do they really mean?
Why did God make some less fortunate than others?
If he wants us to all live in harmony,
Why are some people horrible and drunks and druggies?

No one actually knows the meaning of life,
But I'm sure one day God will invent one extremely able
Person to find it out for us all to know!

Emma Suitor (11)
St Joseph's Catholic High School, Business & Enterprise College, Workington

We Can All Make A Difference

Tick-tock the clock keeps ticking . . .

Monday, I'm watching TV. A boy in Africa has died of AIDS.
I don't know him; who am I to care, his memory will soon fade?

Tuesday, I read a tsunami has washed a village completely away.
Who cares if it's gone. No one visited there anyway.

Wednesday, I heard that in London last night, a riot broke out:
Black vs white.
Asians, black, brown or white. It doesn't bother me if they want to fight.

Thursday, Animal Planet on TV shows a polar bear floating on the ice.
Polar bears are fluffy, animals are cute. It worries me, this isn't nice.

Friday, pollution and war are killing the planet we love.
What can we do to help? We need to know how we can change.

Saturday, 4x4 gone, bottles recycled, donations given,
more thought taken.
I think about Africa, village swept away, these are the changes
I am making.

Sunday, I've realised we can all make a difference and work together
to put it right.
If people cooperate all over the world, we'll make our future safe
and bright.

Georgia Dickinson (11)
St Joseph's Catholic High School, Business & Enterprise College, Workington

Through The Eyes Of The Sea

I am sometimes green, blue or clear,
I am as peaceful as a flower or as fierce as a tiger.
I am inhabited by lots of creatures.
I am the sea.

I am the giver of life,
I am the bringer of death.
I can be smooth or rough,
I am the sea.

I can destroy homes,
I can sink boats.
I can be in or out,
I am the sea.

I give food,
I run through some countries.
I am salty.
I am the sea.

Joshua Jardine (11)
St Joseph's Catholic High School, Business & Enterprise College, Workington

Young Today

Young these days,
They think our minds are trapped in a maze
But we know things even before we talk,
And hey we learnt how to walk,
So why can't you trust us to do our own things.
In the past there were kids who were kings,
Just because one child does something bad you think we all will,
Let us go our own way up this struggling hill.
You don't have to watch every move we make,
We will choose the path we take,
We could make the world a better place,
Just look at our face.
Why do you judge a book by its cover?
And always blame the child's mother,
There are smart kids out there but you won't give us a chance,
Just let loose, enjoy yourself and dance.
We've all got to run while we're young,
So just trust us and be all for one,
Because before you know it everything will be gone.

Hannah Aitken (12)
St Joseph's Catholic High School, Business & Enterprise College, Workington

My Generation

mp3s, PSPs, whatever next?
A levels, GCSEs, or sending a quick text.
I've got to act sharp, it's a fast old world,
Mum's records and player have long-gone been hurled.

Pollution, discharges, nuclear power,
Everywhere you look they're building a tower.
Soldiers at war that's a dead cert,
E numbers are killing my chocolate dessert.

Fossil fuel from pits we are asked not to burn,
Smog, carbon emissions, there's a whole lot to learn.
Ice caps are melting, what no more snow?
Where will the polar bears eventually go?

This global warming what a serious threat,
It wasn't like that in Great Gran's day I bet.
Take plenty of exercise - don't jump in the car,
Cycle or run, it isn't that far!

'Recycle, recycle' shouts Wendy my friend,
There's too much packaging where will it end.
Choking fuel spews from the gas guzzling car,
Polluting the air whilst not moving too far.

There's drugs, guns and crime just down our back street,
With police unaware while patrolling their beat.
I'm only twelve and growing up fast,
Please slow down, I need it to last.

Bullies in the playground they are letting down the schools,
Haven't they heard they're breaking all the rules?
Things sounded so simple in Great Gran's day,
Like country walks and bringing in hay.

I've now much to think about, so little time,
Has there ever been a generation quicker than mine?

Hagen Moss (12)
Ullswater Community College

My Generation Poem!

In my generation you feel modern,
Like you're the king of the world,
You feel great with modern technology,
Like you have power to everyone,
You feel great with iPods,
You feel fantastic with a computer.

My generation will be odd to older generations,
My generation has a bigger complexity,
My generation has more advantages,
Life is worth living in this
Generation.

Kieran Birkett (11)
Ullswater Community College

My Generation Poem!

My generation is the best,
'Cause the most we do is talk and text.

We run and jump and scream and shout,
But over there in Africa they are in a drought.

We do all we can but all we can is not enough,
We live in pleasure but their life is tough.

We go to school and get taught,
But they stay at home and get nought.

For us awesome opportunities abound,
In almost every place they are found.

Tennis, golf, cricket and swimming,
Drama, ballet, dance and singing.

At our doorstep lays a world of ambitions,
All we need to do is take that step, make that mission.

Holly Streatfield (11)
Ullswater Community College

My Generation

What is the one thing we have in our generation?

We live among them they are either our friends or our enemies we build
them or buy them,
They are machines we love them

They can be cold, warm, soft, hard, red, black or silver,
They are machines we love them

They can come in lots of shapes and sizes and can be used for lots of
things, cooking, playing, dancing, running, driving
They are machines we love them

But do we love them? Do we realise what some can do?
Cars chugging out fumes
Boats polluting the seas
Chainsaws slashing down trees

We control the machines and we love them
But do we control the damage too?

Machines are the one thing we have in our generation.

Connie Dalton (11)
Ullswater Community College

My Generation

Tell me how would you like to be a tiger?
More being killed every day,
Being used for pills and medicines,
So would you like that? No way.

Tell me how would you like to be a snow leopard?
Bounding through cliffs and rocks,
Being hunted for your beautiful fur and all,
With only 300 left in Nepal,
Now tell me would you like that?

How would you like to be endangered?
One of the creatures who feels on their own.
Well would you like that?
To be captured or killed any day?
Would you like that?
No way.

Anya Wilcock (11)
Ullswater Community College

My Generation

You don't know how things are these days

Music is better
Designer clothes more comfier
Bikes are classier
Technology is leaving old people behind

Worry about people going to war
Worry about gang activity

Everybody's different
Life can be so mean
Some people don't have anything but the clothes on their back
And a cardboard box
Other people have everything - posh houses, luxury cars
And a swimming pool full of money

You don't know how things work these days
Kids have to stick up for themselves
It's a lot harder to be understood.

That's how it is for kids these days.

Adam Weir (11)
Ullswater Community College

My Generation Poem

M is for modern technology, I have a PSP and an Xbox
Y is for years to come, I want to be a guitarist

G is for grandparents, they care about me
E is for education, I like to learn
N is for new guitar, that's what I'm saving up for
E is for environment that we need to care for
R is for Ross, which is my name
A is for age, I am getting older as generations pass
T is for time that passes quickly
I is for impress, I'm always trying my hardest
O is for older people, we need their experiences
N is for now, the present is important.

Ross Kirkbride (11)
Ullswater Community College

Life As A Refugee

All alone in England,
What am I doing here?
Although I have to admit,
It beats living in fear.
There's war in my country,
Half my family's dead.
Yet here's me in London,
In this warm bed.
I have to live a world of lies,
I've very tired of wiping my eyes.
I wish I wasn't a refugee,
Are there others, just like me?
I try to call, the line is dead.
'Don't bother' is what the others said.
I have to stay strong for now,
But I guess I just don't know how.

Katharine Barnes (12)
Ullswater Community College

Under The Helmet

Every day I walk out there,
I don't know why I do it,
What did they ever do wrong?
By the way, bullets aren't my favourite song.

Lives just lost, because of one man,
But it's not their fault it's ours,
Why do we have to do this?
By the way, bullets aren't my favourite song.

So peaceful people they are,
They're not dangerous or a threat,
But we still keep going because they want something.
By the way, bullets aren't my favourite song.

They think it's their fault,
But we can't blame or we'll be the same,
Not a person, a thing, a problem.
By the way, bullets aren't my favourite song.

Ryan Martin (12)
Ullswater Community College

Burma

We all have to fight
We don't want to die
It's not right
The soldiers tell a lie,
We follow our king
We all don't agree
It's starting to sting
We are forced to flee
The monks are surrounded
We are all sad
They stay bounded
This is bad
Some of us are young
Lives have been lost
We think this war smells like dung
This is going to cost.

Thomas Hemsley (12)
Ullswater Community College

Me A Refugee

London is a map of the universe to me
London snakes like a python's whip to me
London is confusing to me, me a refugee.

People in London are cruel to me,
People in London blame me,
People in London predict me, me a refugee.

The language in London is new to me,
The language is foreign to me,
The language of London is not comforting to me, me a refugee.

Ross Jackson (13)
Ullswater Community College

The Refugee Scar

The future will be bright and better than now,
But I will still bear the scars of injustice.
How I was driven away from my home,
An immigrant to a foreign place.

London, the strange large city of
Dirty back alleys and confusing places.
The people are aloof and block their feelings
With the blank faces of deceased humans.

You will always be alone, a refugee
Never a friend, always an outcast.
A foreign animal, not needed or loved,
An illegal immigrant nowhere is home.

This is the refugee's scar.

Harriet Moar-Smith (12)
Ullswater Community College

My Generation

My generation is full of phones
My generation is full of homes

My generation is going more green
My generation is getting more clean

My generation has no canes
My generation has transport like planes

My generation is cutting down trees
My generation has yummy food like peas

My generation has lots of love
My generation has birds like doves

My generation has rich film stars
My generation may have people living on Mars

When you think of all these things
Is our world really clean?
Is there really lots of love?
Is our world going more green?
I hope so
But the answer's I don't know
It's all up to my generation!

Eve Melling (11)
Ullswater Community College

Alone

Mama is gone, I am scared and frightened.
I must leave my country, Nigeria.
I have been left with only my brother.
We are frightened wandering London's streets.
London people are unfriendly to me.
We are wrongly accused, the police question.
They take us to a social care worker.
I know we will be questioned, soon enough.
He takes us to a block of shabby flats.
We follow him up the dark smelly stairs.
He knocks on a door, a woman answers.
I walk in, he tells us we will be safe.
The lady seems quite nice, I think she cares.
Her son stands up slowly and starts to stare.

Jenna Trelease (12)
Ullswater Community College

Rock, Paper, Scissors

Injustice, a game, rock . . . paper . . . scissors,
A sheet of paper wrapped around the world.
Small, uncovered countries have light of hope.
Black, large paper swarms the rest of the world.
Families hope, pray for the light of peace.
Racism, corruption, no room for joy.
Refugees all alone, no one to help,
Separation of families and children.
Danger! Danger! War around all the world,
Families' dreams are broken and lives lost.
Everything needs to stop we need the hope,
What to do? How to sort out this problem?

Scissors are needed to cut down the black,
Freedom . . . defend the world, don't turn your back.

Sophie McCandlish (12)
Ullswater Community College

If I Could Change The World

If I could change the world
I'd bring my mama back
I miss her very much
I need her guidance, to keep on track

Now! If I could change the world
There would be no famine and no war
I cannot stand much violence
And I hate to see people poor

If I could change the world
No bullying there would be
I really have the nastiness
When I see it, it hurts me.

Emma Edgar (13)
Ullswater Community College

What We Are Not

We are not animals,
We are not sheep,
We are not toys,
That you throw out, or keep

We are people,
Living things,
So why are you any better?
You don't have wings.

We are all equal,
No matter what race,
Look at my eyes,
Look at my face.

Why are we not the same?
Why are we not equal?

Viv Walker (12)
Ullswater Community College

This Is My Life, This Is How I Live It

This is my life, this is how I live it.
Whether I'm British, Polish or religious
People should not dismiss it.

This is my life, this is how I live it
Whether I'm black or white,
Refugee or asylum seeker,
People should not dismiss it.

This is my life, this is how I live it,
Whether I'm on benefits,
Committed a crime
Or not quite with it.
People should not dismiss it.

Sarah Ann Kidd (13)
Ullswater Community College

Young Writers Information

We hope you have enjoyed reading this book - and that you will continue to enjoy it in the coming years.

If you like reading and writing poetry drop us a line, or give us a call, and we'll send you a free information pack.

Alternatively if you would like to order further copies of this book or any of our other titles, then please give us a call or log onto our website at www.youngwriters.co.uk

**Young Writers Information
Remus House
Coltsfoot Drive
Peterborough
PE2 9JX**

(01733) 890066